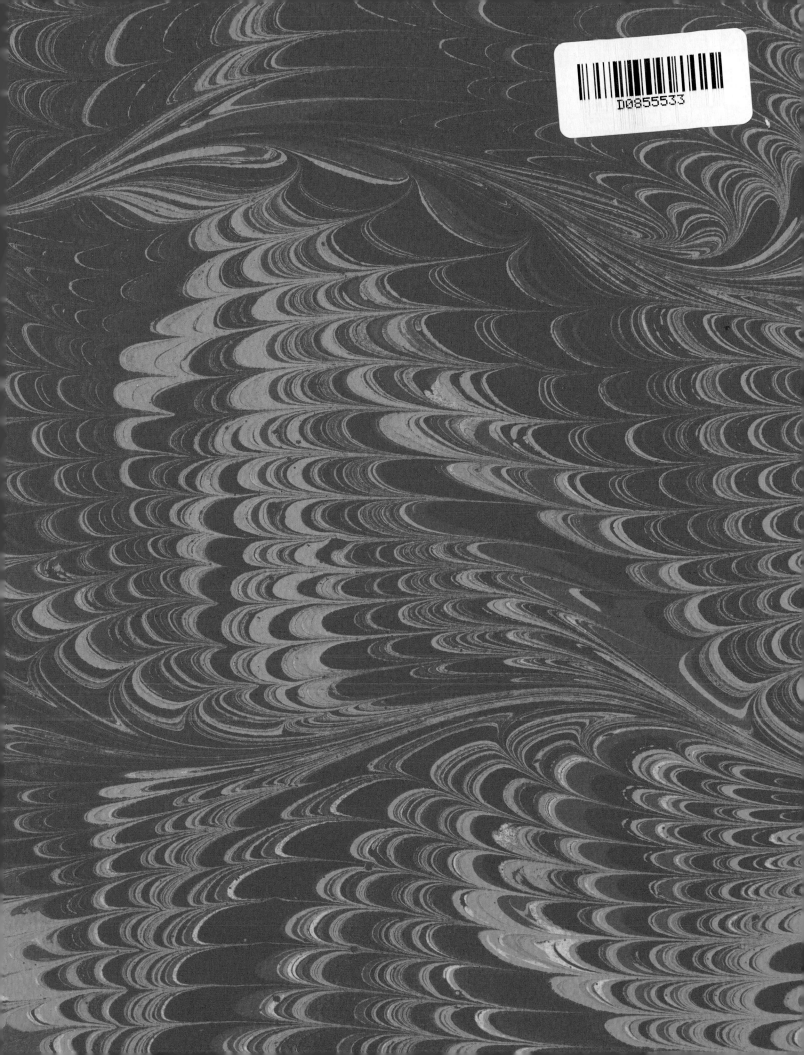

THOMAS JEFFERSON AT MONTICELLO

Edited by

LESLIE GREENE BOWMAN

CHARLOTTE MOSS

Photography by

MIGUEL FLORES-VIANNA

Contributions by

ANNETTE GORDON-REED

CARLA HAYDEN

JAY McINERNEY

JON MEACHAM

XAVIER F. SALOMON

GIL SCHAFER III

ALICE WATERS

THOMAS WOLTZ

THOMAS JEFFERSON AT

MONTICELLO

ARCHITECTURE · LANDSCAPE · COLLECTIONS
BOOKS · FOOD · WINE

CONTENTS

ON A LITTLE MOUNTAIN
IN CHARLOTTESVILLE

Leslie Greene Bowman

S a UNESCO World Heritage Site, Monticello is recognized as a "masterpiece of human creative genius."[1] This book is about Thomas Jefferson's dedication to the arts at Monticello, to the "irreplaceable act of looking,"[2] to the pursuit of a cultivated life uniting the useful and the beautiful, and to the advancement of a young and raw society. Born in provincial central Virginia in 1743, Jefferson was self-taught as an architect, and as a connoisseur. His tutors were his books and his senses, and he accorded each a powerful role in his life. He courted his wife, Martha Wayles Skelton Jefferson, with music; once married they enjoyed literature and duets on keyboard and strings; on her deathbed they recited their favorite verse. Jefferson infused his life with the arts; he expressed the intensity of his feelings with the power of his pen. And for more than five decades, he refined those sensibilities through his creation of an extraordinary laboratory for living, on the top of a little mountain in Charlottesville, Virginia—a plantation he called Monticello.

Annette Gordon-Reed has observed that Monticello represents the best and worst of America[3]—a place to honor the impact of the founder who gave us a mission statement of freedom and equality, and to confront that same man's ownership of six hundred human beings. She has further remarked upon the contrast between Monticello's stunning beauty and the horrors of slavery.[4]

Like the Pyramids, the Parthenon, the Great Wall of China, and countless other sites honored for their cultural significance, Monticello was made possible by enslaved laborers and artisans. Dedicated scholars and interpreters have worked to ensure that every visitor to Monticello today understands its historical reality as a slave plantation and the site's embodiment of the fundamental paradox created at the nation's founding.

If this book captures the vision and connoisseurship of Thomas Jefferson, then it also honors the talents of those in bondage who made every art form at Monticello possible—men, women, and children such as Burwell Colbert, Jupiter Evans, Edith Hern Fossett, John and Priscilla Hemmings, Frances Hern, Wormley Hughes, Isaac Granger Jefferson, and Israel Gillette Jefferson, to name but a few. Whether by building, carving, forging, digging, planting, cooking, polishing, or serving in a myriad of ways, it is they who gave life to Jefferson's vision and designs, who labored long hours, and who deserve recognition for the quality of their creations.

Thomas Jefferson consciously "planted the arts" in our young and fragile country,[5] understanding that the democracy born of revolution was itself insufficient to found a civilization. He ordered an 800-foot mountain cleared and reshaped to create his plantation; no detail escaped his eye. Monticello is much

PAGE 6
With its surmounting dome, the Southwest Portico distinguishes the iconic "nickel" view of Monticello and provided an elegant outdoor sitting room with views of Jefferson's artfully crafted landscape.

RIGHT
Carved by John Hemmings for his wife, Priscilla, this slate headstone was found in the woods of Monticello in the 1950s, sadly separated from her undiscovered grave. It reads: "THE SED [*sic*] IS PLACED AT THE HED OF MY DEAR AFFECTIONAT WIFE PRISCILLA HEMMINGS DEPARTED THIS LIFE ON FRIDAY THE 7TH OF MAY 1830."

more than a house. It was his autobiography, his livelihood, his solace, and his tutorial for peers and posterity on the role of the arts in a civilized nation. Jefferson believed in progress and change through education, and he understood the arts to be a fundamental aspect of that advancement.

In these pages we have invited Jefferson's modern-day cultural peers to remark upon his contributions and the enduring influence of those achievements today. We are indebted to two Pulitzer Prize–winning Jefferson historians for offering us introductory and summary thoughts on how to approach, and what to make of, Thomas Jefferson. We have focused on the natural and material culture of Monticello so as to visually engage the reader with the spectrum of his connoisseurship. I own that we are missing one art form dear to Jefferson—music. He described it as a "favorite passion of my soul" and mourned that "fortune has cast my lot in a country where it is in a state of deplorable barbarism."[6] Jefferson played the violin; he bought his young wife, Martha, a fortepiano. He insisted that his daughters play; at Monticello he supplied each with a harpsichord, and while in Paris, a fortepiano. He hummed and whistled while he worked in his study. We beg the reader to "listen" for that music as they savor Jefferson's other achievements.

This book is really two books on the arts. Even as it explores its subject—Jefferson as a founding visionary and connoisseur—it reveals the genius of another eye, that of the world-renowned art photographer Miguel Flores-Vianna. With Monticello as his canvas, Flores-Vianna shows us the art of seeing and composing, delighting, just as did Jefferson, in the soul-inspiring power of the arts.

1   International Council on Monuments and Sites, *World Heritage List Advisory Body Notification: Monticello and the University of Virginia in Charlottesville* (Charlottesville, VA: United Nations Educational, Scientific, and Cultural Organization and the World Heritage Convention, 1986).

2   Gil Schafer III, "The Perfect and the Personal," in this volume, 54.

3   Annette Gordon-Reed, *The Hemingses of Monticello: An American Story* (New York: W. W. Norton & Company, 2008), 32.

4   Annette Gordon-Reed, comments in a meeting of Monticello's Advisory Committee for African American Affairs (December 12, 2015, Monticello).

5   Benjamin Henry Latrobe to Thomas Jefferson, August 13, 1807, Thomas Jefferson Papers, Library of Congress, Washington, D.C.

6   Thomas Jefferson to Giovanni Fabbroni, June 8, 1778, in *The Papers of Thomas Jefferson*, ed. Julian P. Boyd (vols. 1–20), Barbara B. Oberg (vols. 29–41), and others (Princeton, NJ: Princeton University Press, 1950–), 2:195–98.

OPPOSITE
Music was an essential part of life at Monticello. Family members played keyboard instruments, violin, guitar, and jaw harp.

INTRODUCTION

STATEMENT FOR A
NEW NATION

Annette Gordon-Reed

riting in 1809 to Benjamin Henry Latrobe to congratulate him on "the successful completion" of his "great arch of the Senate Chamber" and "the Hall of Justice" in the Capitol building in Washington, D.C., Thomas Jefferson referred to his home Monticello as his own "essay in Architecture" that he wished his friend Latrobe would visit. Unlike Jefferson, Latrobe had been trained as an architect, and one wonders whether Jefferson used the word "essay," which is one synonym for "attempt," in a self-deprecatory or politely deferential way to acknowledge who between the two of them was the professional architect. Indeed, should Latrobe visit, Jefferson hastens to warn, his essay could be "liable to some unfavorable & just criticisms." Jefferson explains that he had "subordinated" the aims of his essay "to the law of convenience" and that changed circumstances required a change in the original design.[1]

Despite these caveats, the letter leaves no doubt about Jefferson's pride in what he had done in creating Monticello and where he had created it. Even if his "essay in Architecture" hadn't reached perfection, he assures Latrobe a visit would still be worthwhile, because "what nature has done for us is sublime & beautiful and unique," so much so that Latrobe would undoubtedly be moved to art, "to take out his pencil" to reproduce the landscape. The only "difficulty would be in the choice between the different scenes."[2] Jefferson had used the word "sublime" to describe the landscape of his mountaintop home twenty-three years earlier in a completely different type of letter: one written to his great friend Maria Cosway

when he was living in Paris and serving as the American minister to France. Speaking of his "own dear Monticello," he asks, "Where has nature spread so rich a mantle under the eye? mountains, forests, rocks, rivers . . . How sublime to look down into the workhouse of nature."[3]

Central to the story of Monticello is that the dream of such a place was first awakened in Jefferson as a boy, living at the foot of the mountain that he climbed, sometimes with friends, as a place of refuge to read or converse. He certainly would not have had a physical example, within eyesight, of a mansion sitting atop a hill. That vision likely came from the books he later read about Italian villas situated on high. It was a spectacularly impractical thing to think of doing; had he not sited the mansion on the mountain and, in later years, merely talked of having wanted to do that, the idea could be discarded as a youthful folly. Living on a mountain posed a number of logistical problems. The peak of the mountain would have to be leveled off. Much of the material for building and furnishing the house would have to be hauled up the mountain. What about keeping a steady supply of water? What about guests? Wasn't it a bit much to ask visitors to make such a trek? I have written in another context that Monticello was the perfect projection of Jefferson's personality. There was a single-mindedness, a focus, that showed itself in his determination to put his house where he put it and, then, to keep working on his essay for decades. For good and ill, he was not one to think in terms of limits when it came to realizing his visions for himself and, perhaps even more importantly, for the country he helped found.

Monticello as it looked, and as it was placed, was meant to be a statement. There was no United States of America when Jefferson first began to think of his home, and not even when he set about building the first version of the mansion. The place where he brought his bride, Martha Wayles Skelton Jefferson, in 1772, was pre-Revolutionary Virginia, and the home was a statement about pre-Revolutionary Jefferson's class, his confident sense of self, and his desire for privacy, as he plied his trade as a lawyer and soon became a father. The second Monticello, begun after his return from France, became a statement for a new nation, one that he wished would take its place among the other great nations of the world. He wanted to make his home an example of what could be achieved in the new country; beauty would be mixed with the utility of science and conveniences achieved with new designs, some brought back from Europe.

The five years Jefferson spent in France gave him ideas about how to make Monticello not just a place for him to live but a place for his visiting fellow countrymen to learn about art, history, music, and science. From the moment he saw what he considered to be the beautiful farmland as he made his way from the port at Le Havre to Paris in 1784, France began to make an indelible impression upon him. He reveled in the beauty of the buildings, the music, the fashion, the food, and the artwork he saw as he traveled throughout Europe. Jefferson aspired to express the finest taste and material culture of the Virginia gentry into which he was born, perhaps more so because of his parents' modest wealth and provincial location. His birthplace, Shadwell, was on the rough western boundary of Virginia's culturally dominant Tidewater region. Accustomed to the comfortable lifestyle of minor aristocracy, Jefferson embraced the cultural tutelage of France. All of this, no doubt, shaped his sense of aesthetics. What things looked like mattered greatly to him. When he returned to the United States, he had Monticello rebuilt.

Although France loomed large as a cultural referent for Jefferson, his fascination with Italy, which began long before he went to France, shaped the

PAGE 12
Visitors arrived at the Northeast Portico where enslaved butler Burwell Colbert would have greeted the many guests who came to meet the "Sage of Monticello."

PAGE 15
Jefferson sited his home on the spine of an old and gentle mountain range that divides Virginia's coastal plain from its western interior. This dramatic view to the east was revealed once the mountaintop site was cleared by enslaved workers.

OPPOSITE
With the privacy of its shuttered "porticles," the Greenhouse was a place of work, study, and experimentation for Jefferson, and home to his pet mockingbird, Dick.

development of his house and the area around it. While in his twenties, he became acquainted with Andrea Palladio's *Four Books of Architecture*, which set forth the rules of Roman classical-style architecture that appealed to Jefferson's love of order and symmetry. Both of his versions of Monticello showed the influence of Palladio. When Jefferson alerted Latrobe to the fact that the "law of convenience" had made him deviate from his essay's precision, he was referring to concessions he made to adapt classical designs to the demands of site, engineering, economy, and comfort. For example, Jefferson placed two small, green "porticles"—enclosed porches with louvered blinds—off of his living quarters on the southern wing of the house even though they upset the Palladian balance of the design. The northern side of the house has no porticles. This concession was needed to ensure his privacy, as ever more people ventured up the mountain to see the president and then the retired statesman.

So much about Monticello is a product of the way Jefferson delighted in the beauty of Old World Europe, first through books about Italy, then from his long sojourn in France—with a much-enjoyed tour of Italy. But as is often the case,

LEFT
While in Paris, Jefferson commissioned and provided designs to Louis Chantrot to make this clock. He mounted it at the foot of his bed and arose each day when the morning light was sufficient to illuminate its dial.

OPPOSITE
The Lewis and Clark expedition collected and shipped a variety of Native-made wares to Jefferson, some of which he installed in the Hall for the benefit of visitors.

his time away from home in these places that he had admired from a distance gave him a renewed appreciation for his native land. He was made very aware while abroad that the newly created United States was not as sophisticated as Europe, but he came to champion what he considered to be the virtues of a people who were up and coming in the world. He filled Monticello with works of art from Europe—paintings and sculptures—side by side with North American fossils and fauna, Native American art and artifacts, maps, and views of American natural wonders. He sought to provide conversation pieces, some of which would refute prevailing European theories of American inferiority, and all of which would educate visitors as they waited to meet with him or have dinner with his family.

These and other of Jefferson's choices suggest that American practicality was to be melded with beauty for beauty's sake. Monticello mansion bears the influence of the Hôtel de Salm, which was being built while Jefferson was in Paris. Writing to his French friend Madame de Tessé in 1787, in words that reveal how much architecture meant to him, he described himself as having been "violently smitten with the building." In that same letter, he talked of another as well, of "gazing whole hours" at the Maison Carrée, a Roman temple in the south of France, "like a lover at his mistress." Jefferson was deliberately invoking the sensual and sexual to suggest the depth of his feelings about beauty expressed through a building. His playful language shows he knew exactly what he was doing. "This, you will say, was a rule, to fall in love with a female beauty: but with a house! It is out of all precedent! No, Madam, it is not without a precedent in my own history."[4] He did not forget his passion for either building. The second version of Monticello, the one that graces the back of the nickel and is known worldwide, was inspired in part by the domed Hôtel de Salm. For the Virginia statehouse in Richmond, Jefferson provided a design that copied the Maison Carrée.

As Jefferson's letters to Latrobe and to Madame de Tessé indicate, Monticello was just part of the presentation of his home on the mountain. Like the Italian villas he admired so much, with their beautiful gardens and vineyards, Monticello was to be a *ferme ornée*, or ornamental farm. It was a working farm, but he wished it to be beautiful at the same time. This was not simply a matter of exploiting the natural beauty of the place. Beauty would be planned: gardens of flowers, fruits, and vegetables. Peach, fig, and mulberry trees arranged just so. When praising a similar type of farm in Italy, in notes prepared for American visitors to Europe, Jefferson marveled that it exhibited "a very rare mixture of the *utile dulci* [the useful and the pleasurable]"[5] that was particularly worthy of Americans' attention. Beauty was important, but it was not enough for people who lived in a country that had much to do to develop itself to its fullest potential. To that end, Jefferson was constantly on the lookout for new plants and crops to develop in America. "The greatest service which can be rendered any country is to add an useful plant to its culture."[6] He famously took matters into his own hands. On a trip through the Piedmont region in Italy, in defiance of the law, he stuffed a local species of rice into his pockets, smuggling it out with the goal of sending it back to the United States. Technology, in service of agricultural improvements, could alter the landscape, adding to its natural beauty. Extolling his son-in-law's introduction of contour plowing to their region, Jefferson declared that "in point of beauty, nothing can exceed that of the waving lines & rows along the face of the hills & vallies."[7]

The project of using his home and lifestyle to elevate the tastes of his fellow Americans extended beyond the look of his farm, house, and the works of art he owned. Jefferson sought a revolution in American habits. He wished

OPPOSITE
Combining the useful and the pleasurable, this arbor of beans invites a stroll along the southwest border of the Vegetable Garden.

his countrymen to drink less hard liquor in favor of wine, believing "no nation is drunken where wine is cheap; and none sober, where the dearness of wine substitutes ardent spirits as the common beverage."[8] To be sure, his elegant and well-stocked wine cellar was for his enjoyment. But he loved presenting his wines, and the French-inspired cuisine paired with them, to visitors to Monticello and to the President's House. He selected one of the men he enslaved, James Hemings, to accompany him to France to learn French cooking, and was never again without a cook or chef so trained. Entertaining in this fashion—fine wines, excellent cuisine—played a serious role in Jefferson's presidency, as he used his dinner parties as part of his political and legislative strategy to advance his plan as president and leader of the Republican Party.

"I cannot live without books,"[9] Jefferson exclaimed to John Adams, explaining why, after he had sold his spectacular library to the government to reestablish the Library of Congress after the British had burned it during the War of 1812, he had started buying books again. Jefferson proclaimed that music was the "favorite passion of my soul,"[10] but books were certainly not far behind. From the days of

LEFT
Jefferson had "an abundance of books," as enslaved servant Isaac Granger Jefferson recalled. "Sometimes he would have twenty of 'em down on the floor at once."

OPPOSITE
The Cabinet, Jefferson's office space, is where he wrote and read, and also relaxed. He took his daily nap on this small sofa, perhaps dozing off while reading.

his youth, he bought and read books compulsively. Books were the only way that Jefferson, living on the periphery of the Western world, could fully connect to contemporary ideas and thoughts. Isaac Granger Jefferson, an enslaved man at Monticello, painted a vivid picture with his recollections of Jefferson in his living quarters: books, closed and open, strewn all around him. If asked a question to which he had no ready answer, Jefferson would look it up in one of the books, Granger said. He shared his library in other ways, inviting young men who aspired to the bar to read law using his books. He allowed visitors, those whom he liked, to have the use of his library during their sojourns at Monticello. Books were his entrée to the world at large, and he wanted them to be so for others.

For all of his energy, for all of his talent and intelligence, Jefferson's vision of his life as gentleman farmer/renaissance man who was, as the phrase goes, "living the Enlightenment" could not have been, and was not, made real all by himself. The boy fascinated by the mountain near his home, the young man who was determined to build his dream home on top of that mountain, relied on enslaved people to help him realize his visions in nearly every aspect of his life. We could start at the most personal level. The domestic workers who prepared his meals, who made sure his clothes were cleaned, who kept his living space in order—things he never had to think about—left him free to engage life to the fullest extent. And these services were provided without having to pay for them. There is no precise way to calculate it, but living at the top of the social pyramid, with enslaved people at the base, almost certainly added to the sense of being a "special" type of person who deserved to be able to do many things. Jefferson's writings betray his ambivalence about this. He understood clearly that slavery was a violation of the human rights of Black people and had deleterious effects upon the whites who enslaved them. *But* it allowed a person who felt compelled to do many, many things to do many, many things.

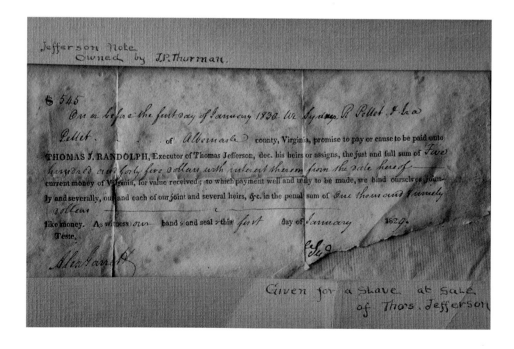

From Monticello's very beginnings, when Jefferson's engagement with the world caused him to create plans that had to be executed, he relied on the enslaved to execute them. Enslaved men and women, hired from nearby, leveled the top of the mountain. They participated in building both versions of Monticello. As the years passed, and Jefferson sought to transform the landscape to make his *ferme ornée*, enslaved men helped him do it. They planted the peach, olive, and fig trees that Jefferson, in letters to others, described himself as having planted, taking the labor of others as his own. And, of course, enslaved people who planted, tended, and harvested crops were the mainstays of the working part of Monticello and other of Jefferson's farms. The enslaved invariably participated in creating the "*utile dulci*" of which Jefferson wrote.

Because of his penchant for order and keeping records, we know the names of some of the enslaved people who were involved in creating the look Jefferson wanted for Monticello. Most of their names are unknown, including those of the children who helped make the bricks to build the second Monticello, some of whose fingerprints can still be seen today. One of the most well-known of his

OPPOSITE
This 1829 promissory note documents the sale of Moses Gillette to two local millers. After Jefferson's death, two auctions separated most of the enslaved families at Monticello, including twenty-three of Gillette's relatives.

RIGHT
Enslaved children were forced to work on the plantation by age ten. Their fingerprints can be found preserved in the bricks they shaped for Monticello's walls.

enslaved workers was John Hemmings[11] who, in the words of Monticello curator Susan Stein, was Jefferson's collaborator. Hemmings was the son of Elizabeth Hemings, the matriarch of the Hemings family, and Joseph Neilson, a white carpenter who worked for a time at Monticello. John Hemmings, a carpenter and joiner as well, made items at Jefferson's request—a fashionable Campeche chair, copies of high-style side chairs, and a landau carriage, among other things. Perhaps because of his parentage, Hemmings was singled out early on by Jefferson to work with wood. Jefferson put him under the direction of two of his white working men, David Watson and James Dinsmore, to learn his craft. In the ensuing decades, working first with Watson and Dinsmore, then alone, Hemmings carried out Jefferson's instructions for building projects at both Monticello and his home away from home, Poplar Forest in Bedford County, ninety miles away from Monticello. There Jefferson employed, on a smaller scale, the principles that had guided his creation of the house and landscape at Monticello.

John Hemmings's connection with Jefferson bore the mark of another aspect of slavery's entanglements. When Hemmings's nephews Beverley, Madison, and Eston were old enough, he was put in charge of them, evidently to prepare them for their lives in freedom when they reached the age of majority, twenty-one. The three were also the sons of Jefferson and Sally Hemings, daughter of Elizabeth Hemings and John Wayles. Every era, and every place, needs people who can build houses and make furniture. By placing his sons with his most favored artisan, the person with whom he worked most often, Jefferson was assured that they would have a marketable skill and that he could supervise their progress through their uncle, John. Indeed, it was Madison Hemings who noted that Jefferson was fonder of being with those who worked on the physical plant of Monticello than dealing with agricultural issues. He certainly rode out and observed enslaved workers in the fields, an activity that seems to have been as much about exercise as anything else. And in later life, he involved himself in gardening, with his white granddaughters and Wormley Hughes, another of Elizabeth Hemings's grandchildren. But over the years, he spent far more time with John Hemmings and, by extension, Hemmings's assistants, Beverley, Madison, and Eston. That Jefferson considered himself handy, making keys and crafting his own pieces of furniture, likely entered into this equation as well. Though he spent most of his time directing others to create beautiful and useful things at Monticello and Poplar Forest, he had a will to attempt this with his own hands.

As is well known, Jefferson's engagement with his *ferme ornée* did not end well for many reasons. Although he loved Monticello, for most of his adult life, another passion competed for his attention. From the days of the American Revolution and through the early republic, the creation of the country, the United States of America, obsessed Jefferson and led him to devote his life to ensuring that this vision of what the country was supposed to be came to fruition. Being minister to France, secretary of state, vice president, and then president took him away from the mountain for long stretches of time. When he finally returned home, he took up another project that had as its ultimate object the improvement of the United States: the creation of the University of Virginia to train young men to be leaders of their state and country. Inattention to the details of the business of farming, his focus on the ornamental aspects of the farm, loans to relatives, and bad economic times ultimately caused his legal family, not long after his death, to lose control of the place he had spent decades building. As traumatic as it was for them, it was even more traumatic for the vast majority of the enslaved people who lived at

Monticello, many of whom had spent more actual time there than Jefferson over the years; 130 of them were put on the auction block seven months after Jefferson died. The house itself had already fallen into disrepair by then, since Jefferson's financial problems had prevented him from doing essential maintenance. Several years later, however, a U.S. naval officer and Jefferson admirer, Uriah Levy, purchased Monticello and set about rescuing it from complete deterioration, setting it on the path to becoming the World Heritage Site it is today: a place that we can safely assume captures Jefferson's dream of an ornamental farm and cultured country seat, though now with extra work required to keep alive the memory of the people enslaved there. All is not lost. In fact, there is much to be gained by seeking to view Monticello through the eyes of the person who first dreamed of making it an example for the nation's cultural aspirations, and through the eyes of those who helped to bring that dream to life, always keeping in mind everything it cost to make that dream real, in human and financial capital.

1   Thomas Jefferson to Benjamin Henry Latrobe, October 10, 1809, in *The Papers of Thomas Jefferson: Retirement Series*, ed. J. Jefferson Looney (Princeton, NJ: Princeton University Press, 2004–), 1:595. Hereafter cited as *PTJ:RS*.

2   Ibid., 1:595–6.

3   Thomas Jefferson to Maria Cosway, October 12, 1786, in *The Papers of Thomas Jefferson*, Julian P. Boyd (vols. 1–20), Barbara B. Oberg (vols. 29–41), and others (Princeton, NJ: Princeton University Press, 1950–), 10:447. Hereafter cited as *PTJ*.

4   Thomas Jefferson to Madame de Tessé, March 20, 1787, in *PTJ*, 11:226.

5   Thomas Jefferson, "Hints to Americans Travelling in Europe," June 19, 1788, in *PTJ*, 13:270.

6   Thomas Jefferson, "Summary of Public Service," [after September 2, 1800], in *PTJ*, 32:124.

7   Thomas Jefferson to Charles Willson Peale, April 17, 1813, in *PTJ:RS*, 6:69.

8   Thomas Jefferson to Jean Guillaume Hyde de Neuville, December 13, 1818, in *PTJ:RS*, 13:490.

9   Thomas Jefferson to John Adams, June 10, 1815, in *PTJ:RS*, 8:523.

10 Thomas Jefferson to Giovanni Fabbroni, June 8, 1778, in *PTJ*, 2:196.

11 The correct spelling of the last name Hemings depends on the family member. Monticello's practice is to use the spelling that the person in question used, if it can be documented. Surviving letters from John Hemmings show his use of the double *m*.

OPPOSITE
The classically proportioned Garden Pavilion, with its sweeping eastern vistas, lies just below Mulberry Row's rough log and frame buildings. Generations later, a descendant of Monticello's enslaved community recalled her grandmother's memories of the beauty of Monticello and the ugliness of slavery.

MONTICELLO

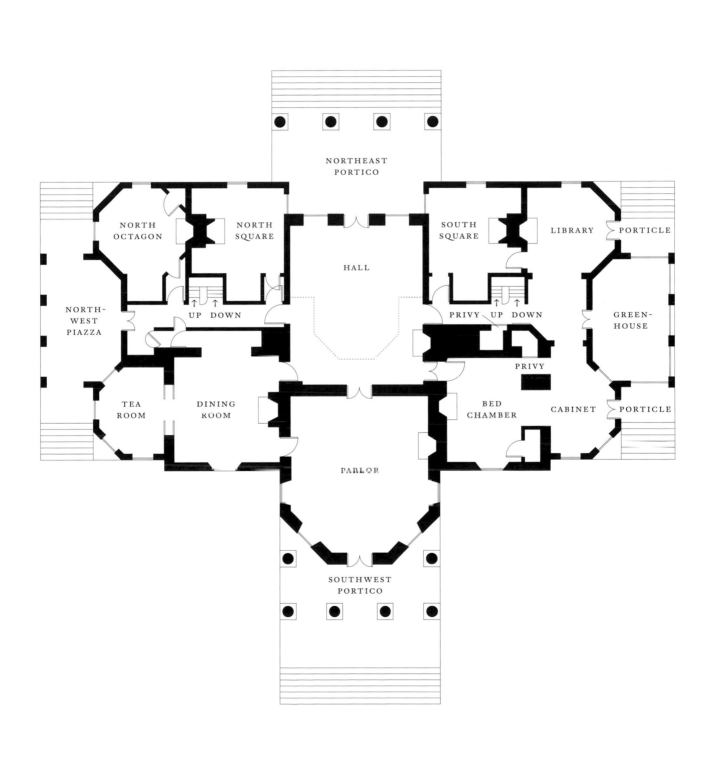

HALL

"THE CHOICEST COLLECTION OF BOOKS"

Carla Hayden

In 2000, we at the Library of Congress celebrated the bicentennial of the nation's library by honoring the individual whose vision inspired and shaped it—Thomas Jefferson. And we did so in a manner that seemed the most fitting tribute: we reconstructed his book collection. Today, the fruits of that effort are ensconced in a pavilion as a permanent exhibition. At its center stands a dramatic circle of tall glass cases that encourages visitors to step in and experience the mind and the world of Jefferson. Surrounded by the impressive scale of his collection—all 6,487 volumes—we are enveloped by his universe, by his world of ideas, by his Enlightenment, which itself constitutes the original foundation of the modern-day Library of Congress.

When we first took on the project to reconstruct Jefferson's 1815 Library, we were certain of our understanding of Jefferson—we knew him as a political thinker, as a president, and as a Virginia planter. Now, more than two decades later, we understand that "knowing" Jefferson is hard work indeed. But over the years, as we have pondered more than six thousand titles that make up his library, we have come to understand the man through his books and his correspondence. An inordinately complex Jefferson emerges—determined, expansive, deliberate, conflicted, engaged, modern, inquisitive, open, and adamant. The legacy of Jefferson, in all its complexity, is to be found in his books.

Jefferson had already acquired a reputation as an authoritative collector and bibliographer by his mid-twenties. Edmund Jennings Randolph, his contemporary and successor as secretary of state, noted that "it constituted a part of Mr. Jefferson's pride to run before

PAGE 44
Jefferson arranged the books in his library by subject, notably History, Philosophy, and Fine Arts, and within each subject by size, from the smallest volumes to the largest folios.

LEFT
Jefferson often marked his books discreetly yet distinctively by adding his initial *T* to the printed signature letter *I* (interchangeable with *J* in early printing), seen here in his copy of Virgil.

OPPOSITE
After the sale of his library to Congress, the avid bibliophile Jefferson replenished his shelves with replacement volumes, including these seventeenth- to nineteenth-century works by Prudentius, Suetonius, La Fontaine, Terence, Ausonius, Ariosto, Tasso, and L'Homond.

the times in which he lived. . . . He had been ambitious to collect a library, not merely amassing [a] *number* of books, but distinguishing authors of merit and assembling them in subordination to every art and science." Even more impressive, Randolph maintained, was the fact that this library presented "to genius the scaffolding upon which its future eminence might be built."[1]

It was a sense of passion and destiny that drove Jefferson to become one of the great eighteenth-century American book collectors. After fifty years of amassing his library, one of the grand monuments to the Enlightenment, it would be this same sense of destiny that led him to respond to the burning of Washington during the War of 1812 by releasing his private collection for the public good. The nucleus of the Library of Congress was forged in that fire. In 1815, Congress purchased Jefferson's personal library—then the largest private book collection in North America—to replace the three-thousand-volume congressional library destroyed when the British burned the U.S. Capitol. Although he faced his own financial difficulties at the time, Jefferson generously offered his entire collection for whatever price Congress deemed appropriate so as to "replace the devastations of British Vandalism."[2]

The collection was, in essence, Jefferson's Enlightenment, his encyclopedia if you will, built on Diderot's prescription "to collect all the knowledge that now lies scattered over the face of the earth, to make known its general structure to the men among [whom] we live, and to transmit it to those who will come after us."[3] Jefferson understood the Enlightenment as a phenomenon of the movement of ideas, propelled by a curiosity about the world and a desire to make it a better place. For him, ideas traveled, above all, through pamphlets and books, implicitly available to a wide audience over space and time.

Jefferson acknowledged that his was likely the largest library available at the time; his great pride in the collection, however, was in the fact that the books it contained had been chosen with great care and discernment.

His endless intellectual curiosity, his worldliness, his keen knowledge of bibliography, his great universal learnedness, and his considerable (though sometimes shaky) means had provided him unique opportunities to acquire a private library that was truly unrivaled in America. This was to become the Library of Congress. This was the collection that had nursed the Declaration of Independence, had guided early American diplomacy, had fueled innovations in American technology, and had assisted a Virginia planter. And now this collection, built around Jefferson's notion of universal knowledge, was to serve as the source of inspiration and ideas for the new republic.

As the collection that Jefferson had built and lived with for nearly fifty years was loaded onto horse-drawn wagons and carted away, he sat down and wrote his friend and agent for the sale of the collection, the newspaperman Samuel H. Smith. It was, he reflected, "unquestionably the choicest collection of books in the US. and I hope it will not be without some general effect on the literature of our country."[4]

Its effect, of course, was profound. Throughout his life, Jefferson gathered books across a vast spectrum of topics and languages. The nation's library today mirrors this universal approach to collecting; the world's largest library is also the only national library that collects internationally in all subjects. Jefferson's strategy for building his library was a practical one. His collection was a working tool rather than a bibliophile's monument. It was the touchstone—the muse for Jefferson the statesman, politician, classicist, inventor, planter, architect, and scientist.

Catastrophic fire again struck the Capitol, on Christmas Eve 1851, destroying two-thirds of Jefferson's original collection. The surviving volumes still serve Jefferson's driving purpose to have the sum of philosophical and practical endeavor readily available. And many of them record Jefferson's discreet ownership mark; he added his initials to complete the printed signatures found in hand-press books from the period. It was with the generous support of Jerry and Gene Jones that, in 1998, we launched the bicentennial project to reconstruct Jefferson's original 1815 collection. An extensive search ensued to find the thousands of volumes that were missing. Some matching editions of those lost to fire were located elsewhere within the library's vast holdings, and the original desiderata of four thousand volumes was whittled down to just over a thousand that would have to be obtained by gift or purchase. That list has since been reduced to the neighborhood of 250

items outstanding. The remaining titles are sought out on the antiquarian market; we are seeking scarce as well as once common, now elusive publications—the arcane as well as the mundane—and in nine different languages from three centuries published in all corners of Europe and the new American republic.

Reconstructing this landmark collection has provided fresh insights into the mind of Jefferson and the world from which he drew his revolutionary ideas. It was the wellspring to one of this nation's deepest thinkers—the drafter of the Declaration of Independence, the third president, and a true visionary who helped mold a new form of government. In the richly ornamented hall of the Library of Congress named in Jefferson's honor, amid the thousands of volumes that comprised his 1815 collection, we can rediscover the dialogue Jefferson carried on with his books—his ideas, his era, and the universe that surrounded him. Perhaps most important, the Jefferson Collection serves as a powerful embodiment of the principle on which the Library has been built—that knowledge and free access to it, by both the leaders and the governed, are essential to democracy.

1   Edmund Jennings Randolph, *History of Virginia*, ed. Arthur H. Shaffer (Charlottesville: University Press of Virginia, 1970), 181–82.

2   Thomas Jefferson to John Adams, June 10, 1815, in *The Papers of Thomas Jefferson: Retirement Series*, ed. J. Jefferson Looney (Princeton, NJ: Princeton University Press, 2004–), 8:523. Hereafter cited as *PTJ:RS*.

3   Denis Diderot, "The Encyclopedia," in *Rameau's Nephew and Other Works*, trans. and ed. Jacques Barzun and Ralph H. Bowen (Indianapolis, IN: Hackett Publishing Company, 2001), 277.

4   Thomas Jefferson to Samuel H. Smith, May 8, 1815, in *PTJ:RS*, 8:476.

OPPOSITE
Some of the library Jefferson collected in retirement he kept in his Bed Chamber, in a narrow bookcase he fashioned for this purpose.

ARCHITECTURE

THE PERFECT
AND THE PERSONAL

Gil Schafer III

Monticello, the home that Thomas Jefferson created from 1768 until 1826 (with time off to write the Declaration of Independence, serve two terms as president, and address various other distractions), remains one of the most studied and written-about private houses in our nation, and there is little I can add to this voluminous scholarship. In short, I'm not an expert. But as an American residential architect working in the classical tradition—as someone who has pondered, admired, and learned from my great predecessor's example, and at times considered my (much more modest) efforts through the prism of Jefferson's experience—I've discovered parallels between his journey and my own that have been personally meaningful, in particular the ways in which the maturity of years and experience impacts creativity.

Each time I visit Monticello, which I do with regularity, I am reminded of the multilayered character of its author's accomplishment. Jefferson often expressed the belief that good architecture could benefit the nation he'd helped to establish. He believed that the arts— of which he professed architecture was the "most important"[1]—were essential to "improve the taste of my countrymen, to increase their reputation, to reconcile them to the respect of the world and procure them it's praise."[2] The architecture of Monticello does all that, without question. But it also achieves something else— something at once more personal and, more particularly, American.

A precocious creator, Jefferson discovered architecture at the College of William & Mary, where, apparently on a whim, he purchased an architectural pattern

PAGE 50
Jefferson used the visually striking Doric order in his design for the porticos. Perhaps Jefferson's favorite, four different versions of this robust order can be seen at Monticello.

LEFT
Jefferson was around thirty years old when he designed these chimneys for the original Monticello. Referencing Palladio's plans for a Doric pedestal and featuring caps and bases carved from local quartzite, they are a poignant expression of the young architect's dedication to faithful interpretation of classical precedent.

OPPOSITE
Despite his love of symmetry, Jefferson had to raise two of the Dome Room's windows, including the one seen on the right, to avoid the abutting roofline.

book from a drunken Williamsburg cabinetmaker. In time, books became essential to his process: throughout his life, Jefferson felt unable to design without them, and *Select Architecture* by Robert Morris, James Gibbs's *Book of Architecture*, and in particular the first of Andrea Palladio's *Four Books of Architecture*—Jefferson's "bible"[3]—powerfully influenced the largely self-taught practitioner.

If imitation is truly the sincerest form of flattery, all three architects would have appreciated Jefferson's first pass at Monticello. He had to start by having the mountaintop leveled, a formidable task achieved by slave labor over several months in 1768 when Jefferson was twenty-five years old. Then work commenced on the south pavilion—a single-room structure measuring 18 by 18 by 18 feet, with a shallow gabled roof. The pavilion was finished two years later. The final design of the main house, arrived at over a long series of iterations and adjusted continually after construction began in 1769, grew from a square into a rectangle and, finally, a cruciform plan

(all indebted to Gibbs) with six-sided "bow" rooms at the north and south ends, and two-story central porticos to the east and west that deviated from Palladian precedent in that both stories were precisely the same height (an idea that, according to the historian Gene Waddell, the magpie Jefferson got from an essay by Francis Bacon).[4] Monticello in its first form featured three grand rooms on the main floor—Jefferson's bed chamber, a parlor, and a dining room—each of which could be accessed via its own door from the open-air "lodge" that formed the house's vestibule. Jefferson equally addressed the site in these early designs: in his planning, Monticello sat at the center of a U-shaped arrangement of walkways that partially enclosed a lawn to the west and terminated in the north and south pavilions.

Jefferson was also a man obsessed with facts and figures—he kept records of the number of bricks required at each stage of construction and calculated dimensions out to multiple decimal points. He recorded the rate at which enslaved laborers could dig cellars, clear and grade roads, cut and split rails, forge nails, and harvest wheat. For the people tasked with this labor, Jefferson's expectations were likely unrealistic. His mathematical exactitude often failed to account for human variation.

With certain exceptions, the first Monticello, which was partially demolished in 1796 when Jefferson began the renovations that created the house we see today, reflects its architect's passion for symmetry, accuracy, and proportion. "Everything worked together, everything was proportional—it was an academic, mathematical exercise,"[5] observes Gardiner Hallock, vice president of architecture, collections, and facilities at Monticello today. It was, to be sure, a remarkable accomplishment: the Marquis de Chastellux, who visited in 1782, noted that Jefferson was "the first American who . . . consulted the Fine Arts to know how he should shelter himself from the weather."[6] Yet the design, begun when Jefferson was in his early twenties, was the work of a gifted amateur, a student who had made an exacting study of his heroes but had yet to come into his own.

One wonders how we'd feel about the original design if it were the one that, since 1938, has famously graced the reverse of the American nickel. But the first Monticello was, in fact, never finished. After his wife died, in 1782, Jefferson went into a depression, and work more or less stopped. Then, in 1784, he was sent to Paris to negotiate treaties with the nations of Europe and North Africa, and subsequently succeeded Benjamin Franklin as minister to France. When he departed, Monticello might have passed for an early example of a downtown loft: paintings and mirrors hung on unplastered interior brick walls.

Jefferson remained in Europe until 1789, and it was there he found his mature style—in large measure through the irreplaceable act of looking. In his half-decade abroad, Jefferson traveled widely, in Italy and England as well as France; seasoned by revolution, political authority, and personal tragedy, his tastes, knowledge, and, not least, his confidence grew. As someone whose own eye and design instincts have also improved with time and travel, I would speculate that what Jefferson saw gave him permission to be less rule-bound—to trust that his sensibilities would let him take liberties without violating his aesthetic principles.

Several things influenced Jefferson in particular. One was his discovery that "all the new and good houses are of a single story."[7] Another was the Hôtel de Salm on the Seine's Left Bank. Home today to the French Legion of Honor, it was constructed as a private residence during Jefferson's stay in Paris, and its dome, massing,

Mr Jefferson

Mr Jefferson

Mr Jefferson
Ministre Plénipotentiaire
des États Unis d'Amérique

and neoclassical reserve impressed him enormously. So did the dome of the Halle aux blés, the circular grain exchange (now the site of the Bourse de commerce). Both buildings, as well as the au courant preference for one-story residences, found their way into the reinvention of Monticello, which began in 1796. In his *History of Virginia*, Edmund Jennings Randolph observed that "it constituted a part of Mr. Jefferson's pride to run before the times in which he lived."[8] This impulse toward the avant-garde is entirely evident in what today is often referred to as "Monticello Two."

Needful of more space; not pleased, speculates Waddell, with "Monticello One's" disproportionate appearance;[9] and desirous of a dwelling that reflected his Continental sensibilities (and social and political standing), Jefferson both compressed the house and thickened it—even though it gained considerable square footage, the subtraction of the double portico paradoxically made Monticello look smaller. Jefferson preserved his three original great rooms, but on the east side he tore off the facade, added a grand entry hall opposite the Parlor, expanded his personal precinct to include a two-room library (to the south), and balanced this with a pair of guest bedrooms (to the north). While the Parlor, Dining Room, and Jefferson's bed chamber retained their original eighteen-foot ceiling heights, the secondary main-floor spaces drop down to ten feet (per the French style); the ceilings fall to eight feet on the second floor and even lower in the garret spaces under the roof.

Though Monticello Two is effectively a three-story house, Jefferson's design cleverly conceals that fact. My favorite device is the setting of some second-story windows at floor height, so that from without they appear to be transoms on the first-story windows directly below them; meanwhile, the balustrades encircling the parapet hide the garret spaces. The trick works—on the eastern facade, at any rate. On the western elevation, the illusion is undercut somewhat by the looming presence of Monticello's signature feature, the dome.

How, precisely, that stunning if hard-to-reach room beneath the iconic dome was meant to be used isn't entirely clear (at Jefferson's death it was a storage room). To me, it's a kind of folly, a permissible indulgence by a man whose aspirations had been inflamed by Parisian peregrinations. Yet the dome is a delight to experience, and it contains some of Jefferson's most adroit design moves. Tasked with fitting an octagon atop a rectangle, he stretched the sidewalls slightly and adjusted the height so that the structure could cohabitate comfortably with the roof line. Jefferson also elevated the two

windows flanking the doorway—they're roughly a foot higher than the others—so as to hide the view of the attic framing (replacing the lower part of the glazing with mirrors as an extra measure). The dome also features a baseboard inspired by Palladio's drawing of the Attic order of the Temple of Nerva Trajan, which is so enormous that it can only be described today as prepostmodern. The architect followed the dictates of necessity and the demands of his heart. The outcome isn't necessarily "correct"—but so what?

While Hallock describes Jefferson as "an innovative collector of ideas rather than an inventor,"[10] one of the joys of experiencing Monticello lies in its spirited embrace of novelty. This begins at the beginning, with the compass on the ceiling of the entry portico that spins in concert with the weathervane above it, and continues above the front door, on the interior, with a wall clock controlled by cannonball-like counterweights. Doors that magically spring open with the twist of a knob continue the amazements, as do the wine dumbwaiters concealed in the dining room mantelpiece. The Parlor's parquet floor—stunningly expensive, diabolically difficult to build—was one of America's first, and there were structural innovations as well: Jefferson's sawtooth roof may have leaked, but the low pitch made it less "offensive to the eye";[11] so-called air closets ventilated the house from the ground floor to the roof. He also tweaked the landscape, moving the Palladian front courtyard to the rear and half-burying the support spaces beneath the terrace decks so that they wouldn't obstruct the views.

Thomas Jefferson was, to be sure, a complicated individual. Like wealthy men before and since, he

OPPOSITE
In the center of the Hall ceiling is a soaring eagle in plaster relief surrounded by eighteen stars, similar to the Great Seal of the United States. The number of stars suggests installation between 1812 and 1816, when states numbered eighteen.

RIGHT
Jefferson was keenly aware of time management. He custom ordered the Great Clock and mounted it over the front door, with a corresponding face on the exterior wall. Its works were connected to a gong on the roof, which sounded the hours across the plantation.

insisted upon having his way, whether that involved settling his entire multifaceted life on a mountaintop—necessitating the near-constant hauling of wagonloads of essentials (including ten cords of wood per month) up steep, winding nineteenth-century roads—or scouring the world to find precisely the right Chinese gong to bong out the hours from Monticello's roof.

And there is the harsh reality that Jefferson's dream house was put together, in large measure, with the labor of enslaved people, many of whom were highly skilled artisans. John Hemmings (1776–1833) was trained by and succeeded the Irish joiner James Dinsmore. Burwell Colbert (1783–1862), Jefferson's personal servant and butler, was also a painter and window glazer for the house. Thrimston Hern was a carpenter and stonecutter. Jupiter (1743–1800), whose last name might have been

Evans and who had known Jefferson since birth and served as his valet in Williamsburg, learned stonemasonry and worked on the columns of the house's east front. Their achievements and those of countless others attest to the reality and horror of slavery, and permeate one's entire experience of Monticello.

Thus, in all of its aspects, Monticello has important lessons to teach—from the profound to the practical. One such lesson is embodied, for me, by Jefferson's famous bed, which sits in a niche that opens to his bed chamber on one side and to his study on the other. Eccentric, yes, but for a reason: so that, upon waking, Jefferson could choose immediately between his personal and professional lives.

My generation of classical architects emerged into a profession dominated by modernists, and at first we

LEFT
The Chinese gong Jefferson imported in the mid-1790s continues to ring out the hours from its rooftop housing. Peter Fossett, born into slavery at Monticello, recalled that it could be heard six miles away.

OPPOSITE
Jefferson derived his elegant designs for the roof balustrade from examples by Andrea Palladio and James Gibbs, but they were brought to life by a talented enslaved woodworker known to posterity only as "Lewis."

stuck close to precedent, and to the rules. But classicism is a language, and as we became conversant with its grammar and syntax, we felt increasingly free to interpret it, to speak in a more personal way. Like Jefferson, when I first built a house of my own, I made a close study of historical precedent, and while my design was driven to a degree by memory, it was rooted firmly in architectural correctness. In the years since, I've allowed instinct and intuition to play a stronger role in my work. And—also like Jefferson—the houses I have built are a reflection not so much of an historical ideal but of who I am. You might say that the Monticello we so admire today reflects that same dichotomy: a place of stunning classical grandeur, exceptional eccentricity, and the seductive tension between the two; it is a conversation between the younger and elder Jeffersons, and a meditation on the strengths of both. There is much that is perfect—but where perfection exists, it's there because it's personal. Therein lies the lesson, whether you're building a home or a life. Follow it, and like the great man himself, you'll never get up on the wrong side of the bed.

Over time I've come to understand that an architect's profession has the power to do more than provide shelter; it has the power to stand for enduring values and ideals. I recognize that aspect of my journey in Jefferson as well. Our third president believed in the power of architecture to elevate his nation, and in the course of a long life—he died on the fiftieth anniversary of the Declaration—he contributed much to the public realm, including the development of the capital and the Olympian campus of the University of Virginia. Surely he thought of Monticello as an emblem of his country's potential. Yet Jefferson's true gift was to create an architecture that personified our great national experiment—indeed, our character: an architecture, like the nation, unafraid to break with the past and one that privileged freedom of expression, both individual and collective.

The American spirit, in three dimensions: that's what you'll find at Monticello.

1   Thomas Jefferson, "Hints to Americans Travelling in Europe," June 19, 1788, in *The Papers of Thomas Jefferson*, ed. Julian P. Boyd (vols. 1–20), Barbara B. Oberg (vols. 29–41), and others (Princeton, NJ: Princeton University Press, 1950–), 13:269. Hereafter cited as *PTJ*.

2   Thomas Jefferson to James Madison, September 20, 1785, in *PTJ*, 8:535.

3   Isaac A. Coles, "Account of a Conversation with Thomas Jefferson," [before February 23, 1816], in *The Papers of Thomas Jefferson: Retirement Series*, ed. J. Jefferson Looney (Princeton, NJ: Princeton University Press, 2004–), 9:500.

4   Gene Waddell, "The First Monticello," *Journal of the Society of Architectural Historians* (University of California Press) 46, no. 1 (March 1987), 16.

5   Gardiner Hallock, interview, January 13, 2020. The author is indebted to Mr. Hallock for this and other insights for this essay, and his deep command of Monticello history.

6   Marquis de Chastellux, *Travels in North America in the Years 1780, 1781, and 1782*, trans. Howard C. Rice, Jr. (Chapel Hill: University of North Carolina Press, 1963), 391.

7   Thomas Jefferson to John Brown, April 5, 1797, in *PTJ*, 29:345.

8   Edmund Jennings Randolph, *History of Virginia*, ed. Arthur H. Shaffer (Charlottesville: University Press of Virginia, 1970), 181.

9   Ibid., 24.

10   Gardiner Hallock, interview, January 13, 2020.

11   Thomas Jefferson to James Dinsmore, January 3, 1803, in *PTJ*, 35:296.

OPPOSITE
Jefferson admired alcove beds in Paris and installed them at Monticello. He opened his own bed both to his chamber and his cabinet, so as to enter either upon waking.

THE PRIVATE SUITE

LIBRARY
CABINET
BED CHAMBER

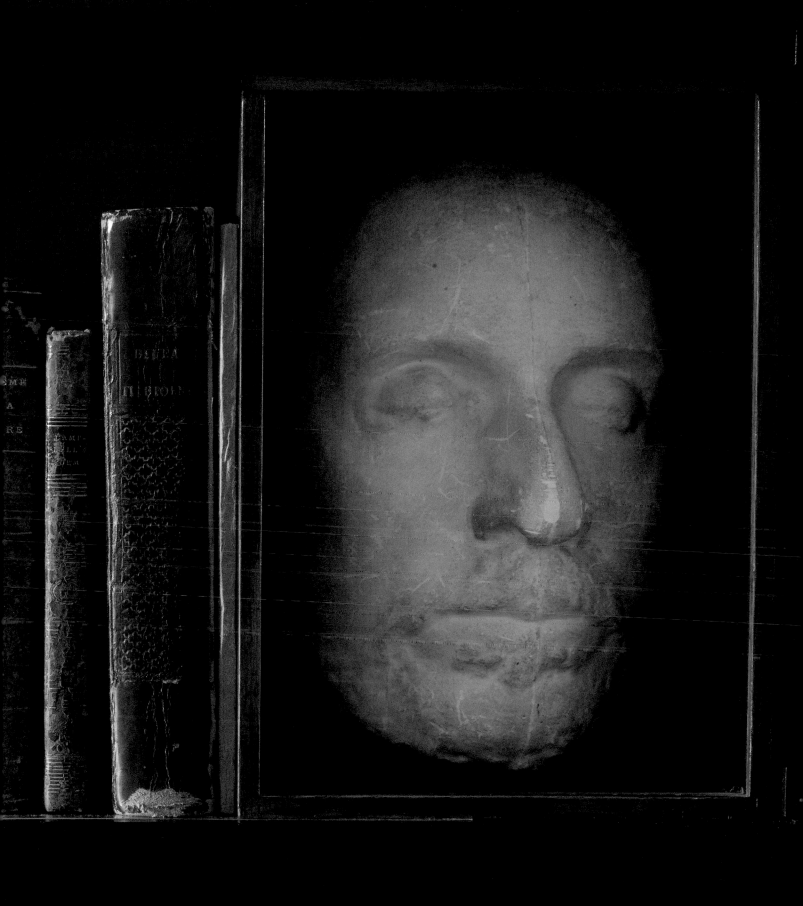

PAGE 65
A bust of James Madison in the east window of the Library gazes on the paper press used to smooth out the tightly folded letters of the day.

PAGES 66–67
The Library as it may have looked after Jefferson sold his books to Congress in 1815.

PAGES 68–69
Once a repository for Jefferson's renowned collection of books, the Library also contained oddities such as the death masks of Oliver Cromwell (seen here) and Sir Isaac Newton.

PAGES 70–71
Adjoining the Bed Chamber and Library, the Cabinet, from the French for "office," was the center of Jefferson's intellectual world and off-limits to most guests.

PAGE 72
A bust of John Adams presides over the filing presses used to archive Jefferson's prodigious correspondence.

PAGE 73
Concave mirrors were vital for scientific experiments because they focused and magnified light, with the unintended consequence of reflecting the image upside down. But they were also a curiosity, and Jefferson later installed this looking glass in the Hall to amuse his guests and family.

PAGE 74
The double-height Bed Chamber features a skylight, bed alcove, and, above the bed, a small upper-story closet with oval openings for ventilation.

PAGE 75
Jefferson designed his personal space for convenience, complete with a remotely operated lock on his chamber door, likely activated from the pull cord next to his bed.

PAGE 76
After Jefferson's years as a fancily dressed American diplomat, he was often described wearing a red waistcoat, undoubtedly referring to this late-eighteenth-century silk crepe and velvet one.

PAGE 77
Small personal objects such as letter openers, drafting instruments, writing sets, and razors bring Jefferson to life, revealing his varied interests and daily habits.

OPPOSITE
Benjamin Tyler's Declaration of Independence was the first decorative print of America's founding document to include facsimiles of the fifty-six signatures. Tyler sent a copy to Jefferson upon publication in 1818.

COLLECTIONS

A MIRROR OF THE WORLD

Xavier F. Salomon

At the heart of Monticello—at the center of the ground-floor plan—is a set of double doors that connects the Hall, the most public room of the house, to the Parlor, where Jefferson and his family entertained their guests with games and music. Flanking the doors on the Parlor side are two matching pier mirrors measuring more than nine feet high. Crafted from pairs of sizable panes and technologically astounding for their time, each mirror is surrounded by a frame itself composed of eighteen smaller mirrors. Unframed mirrors were among the objects included in a shipment of crates that Jefferson had sent from France in 1790, after the start of the French Revolution, as the world of the ancien régime, of which he had witnessed the splendid twilight, was rapidly drawing to an end. Between 1784 and 1789, Jefferson had served diplomatically in Paris, where he established his residence at the Hôtel de Langeac. Since King Louis XIV had installed his spectacular Galerie des Glaces at Versailles in the early 1680s, mirrors had become a status symbol, one that featured in every elegant Parisian home.

There was a variety of mirrors in a number of rooms at Monticello, and while some came from France, others were acquired or framed in America. Jefferson's large pier mirrors reflect Monticello's spacious Parlor—its furniture, paintings, and musical instruments—as well as the landscape outside the west garden front, including the foothills of the Blue Ridge Mountains. The mirrors covered empty niches that were vestiges of Jefferson's first version of Monticello—intended for copies of classical sculptures. This simple wall divided by a door embodies important aspects of Jefferson as a collector. The ambitious Virginia politician and scholar was enamored with antiquity and created a building and its contents based on the translation of edifices and sculptures he knew only through books. In the same way in which the first Monticello was the result of Jefferson's knowledge of Palladian architecture through the volumes of his library, the sculptures he originally envisioned for his house were copies of celebrated classical antiquities that he never saw, such as the Apollo Belvedere and the Farnese Hercules. The list of sculptures he wanted for Monticello, as documented around 1771, was entirely based on second-hand knowledge, mainly on Joseph Spence's *Polymetis,* first published in 1747. However, the Jefferson who returned to Virginia in 1789, after five years in France with sojourns to Italy and England, was the founding father who, more than any other, had engaged with the culture and arts of what he defined as the United States' "transatlantic brethren."[1]

He changed the architecture at Monticello substantially, but he also, over the years, moved many objects and artworks in and out of the house and among its various rooms. The mirrors at Monticello reflect their ever-shifting surroundings and echo through their surfaces the art and nature within and around the home. The house itself mirrors Jefferson's curiosity and myriad interests, as well as his incessant pursuit of knowledge and his ambition to advance culture in the fledgling nation he had been instrumental in creating.[2]

While in Paris, in 1785, Jefferson wrote to James Madison, "You see I am an enthusiast on the subject of the arts. But it is an enthusiasm of which I am not ashamed, as its object is to improve the taste of my countrymen, to increase their reputation, to reconcile them to the respect of the world and procure them its praise."[3] In the nascent republic, art was viewed with a certain amount of suspicion because of its inherent links to European royalty and aristocracy, but throughout his life Jefferson defended the significance of the arts and their potential to improve humankind.

As Jefferson was creating Monticello, he was bringing to Virginia what he believed to be the best that Europe had to offer: from the architectural language of Palladio and sixteenth-century Veneto to the wooden parquet floors masterfully based on French examples he had seen in Paris. He had an astounding ability to focus on both the large picture and the details, and his correspondence teems with information on every aspect of human knowledge. His purchases and commissions for Monticello fall into two broad, occasionally overlapping categories: functional objects for everyday use and the

LEFT
The Great Clock's cannonball weights descend to mark the day of the week, under the gaze of Jefferson's adversary Alexander Hamilton.

OPPOSITE
When Jefferson received a pair of pre-Columbian, Mississippian-era figures (one of which is seen here), he lauded them as "monuments to the state of the arts among the Indians."

more proper collection of artifacts whose main purpose was their display for the enjoyment and edification of not only Jefferson's family but also his many guests.

The furniture at Monticello is a combination of American and European objects. Jefferson owned tables and chairs created by American craftsmen in Philadelphia and New York, as well as pieces acquired in Paris during the second half of the 1780s and, to a lesser degree, on his visit to London in April 1786. Many of these objects were purchased not only for their elegance but also for their technological innovation. No house in Virginia, and few in America, for instance, would have had mirrors on the scale of Jefferson's pier mirrors. He also gathered the latest European contraptions, such as the drafting table designed by Denis-Louis Ancellet. Furniture was still arriving at Monticello from Paris

years after its master had returned from Europe; for example, the suite of *fauteuils à la reine* with saber legs attributed to Georges Jacob was delivered after 1815.

Jefferson routinely relied on the proficient enslaved craftsmen in the joiner's shop at Monticello, and a number of pieces of furniture in the house were built, following Jefferson's designs and suggestions, by John Hemmings. Under one roof, then, could be found chairs made by the most celebrated *menuisier* of King Louis XVI and Marie Antoinette, settees in the Etruscan style sourced from Philadelphia, and Campeche chairs (or "siesta chairs" as Jefferson sometimes called them), made by the enslaved cabinetmaker active in a workshop on Mulberry Row. This encapsulates Jefferson's taste, which was at once eclectic, practical, and sophisticated. He acquired lavish everyday objects (such

as clocks or a silver coffee urn accompanied by East India porcelain tea, coffee, and chocolate cups) but also designed many objects himself. In 1789, while in Paris, he commissioned silversmith Claude-Nicolas Delanoy to execute his design for a pair of silver-and-vermeil goblets. Jefferson also adapted or copied designs seen in his travels. Back in the United States, he ordered a set of silver tumblers, based on a French example in his possession, from John Letelier, a silversmith in Richmond. The most refined of copies is the silver *askos* (a pouring vessel) made for Jefferson by Simmons and Alexander in 1801, precisely following the model, provided by the president, of an ancient bronze artifact he had seen in Nîmes in 1787.

The architect Benjamin Henry Latrobe wrote to Jefferson in 1807, praising him as the man responsible for having "planted the arts in your country."[4] When Jefferson returned from France, he was followed by a number of paintings he had acquired in Paris. Jefferson visited some of the most important collections of artworks in Europe at the time, but he did not have the means to acquire significant works by contemporary artists. He admired Jacques-Louis David's *Death of Socrates* at the Salon of 1787, for example, but paintings of that quality were beyond his reach. The canvases sent to Monticello from Paris were mostly copies of Old Masters—artists particularly celebrated at that time such as Raphael, Titian, and Domenichino, as well as Jefferson's favorite, Guido Reni, of whose work he owned six copies. These were accompanied by copies after Northern European painters such as Frans Floris, Jan Gossaert, and Hendrick Goltzius. It seems that these copies were often acquired more for their subject matter—classical and biblical—than for their intrinsic artistic merits. On the walls of Monticello, Jefferson displayed European images to which his compatriots would not otherwise have had access. It is useful to recall here that the first museums in America were largely filled with copies of European masterpieces and casts of classical sculptures.

Portraiture was particularly important for Jefferson. Through the Florentine physician and merchant Philip Mazzei, he acquired copies of portraits from the Uffizi in Florence of four figures linked to American history: Christopher Columbus, Amerigo Vespucci, Ferdinand Magellan, and Hernán Cortés. To these, he added a picture of Sir Walter Raleigh. These portraits shared the walls of the Parlor with likenesses of "the three greatest men that have ever lived," according to Jefferson[5]—Francis Bacon, Isaac Newton, and

OPPOSITE
When in France, Jefferson commissioned a wooden copy of a Roman *askos*, or pitcher, shown left here, which he used as a model for the silver version he ordered from Philadelphia in 1801.

John Locke—and a number of Jefferson's contemporaries: George Washington, Benjamin Franklin, John Adams, the Marquis de Lafayette, John Paul Jones, James Madison, and Thomas Paine. His interest in portraiture also extended to sculpture. While in Paris, he had met Jean-Antoine Houdon, France's most celebrated sculptor at the time, and had sat for him. Later, in 1785, Jefferson was instrumental in facilitating Houdon's short trip to America to portray Washington in a full-length sculpture for the Virginia statehouse—a building that also resulted from Jefferson's influence, adapted from plans he had commissioned of the Maison Carrée in Nîmes, France. At Monticello, he displayed six terracotta-patinated plaster busts after Houdon's marbles: four in the Tea Room (Washington, Lafayette, John Paul Jones, and Franklin) and two in the Hall (Turgot and Voltaire). Giuseppe Ceracchi portrayed Jefferson during one of the Italian sculptor's two American sojourns, and two of Ceracchi's works (busts of Jefferson and Hamilton) were displayed in the Hall. Although Jefferson never met the artist or saw his work

firsthand, he was also responsible for the creation of Antonio Canova's only work destined for the United States: a life-size marble statue of Washington for the statehouse in Raleigh, North Carolina, sadly lost in a fire in 1831.

The collection of paintings and sculptures at Monticello was not limited to works by European artists. Portraits of important American leaders were accompanied by images, especially in the Dining Room, of sites in this country by American artists; the wonder of nature was always a central interest for Jefferson. Paintings of local sites, such as the junction of the Potomac and Shenandoah rivers, and the Natural Bridge, lyrically described by Jefferson in his *Notes on the State of Virginia*, were displayed with paintings of Niagara Falls. As reflected in the mirrors in the Parlor, the landscape of Virginia, and of America in general, was brought into the house not only from the expansive windows of Monticello but also through these paintings and prints. Jefferson's collecting practice was also very much directed to other fields linked to the natural world, such as maps, scientific instruments, and even plants and seeds for his gardens.

The most extraordinary space in Monticello, in terms of the objects assembled for it, is the Hall, which Jefferson envisaged as an "Indian Hall." This was the space in which every visitor to the house would be welcomed. In 1815, George Ticknor wrote:

> You enter, by a glass folding-door, into a hall. . . . On one side hang the head and horns of an elk, a deer, and a buffalo; another is covered with curiosities which Lewis and Clarke found in their wild and perilous expedition. On the third, among many other striking matters, was the head of a mammoth, or, as Cuvier calls it, a mastodon, containing the

only *os frontis*, Mr. Jefferson tells me, that has yet been found. On the fourth side, in odd union with a fine painting of the Repentance of Saint Peter, is an Indian map on leather, of the southern waters of the Missouri, and an Indian representation of a bloody battle, handed down in their traditions.[6]

Ceracchi's and Houdon's busts, together with Old Master copies and a marble version of the classical Sleeping Ariadne, were shown alongside Native American art and artifacts, both ancient and contemporary, animal fossils, and other natural history specimens. Already by 1809, Jefferson owned two Mississippian soapstone figures: "two busts of Indian figures male and female by Indians in hard stone . . . they were dug up at a place

OPPOSITE
In the Tea Room, Jefferson assembled his "most honorable suite"—portrait busts of American Revolutionary heroes by his favorite sculptor, Jean-Antoine Houdon. Seen here, from left to right, are John Paul Jones, Benjamin Franklin, and George Washington.

RIGHT
In the Hall, Jefferson's guests were greeted with rare and extraordinary artifacts, such as the painted Mandan buffalo robe depicting an important battle between the Mandan and the Sioux and Arikara peoples.

called Palmyra, on the Tennissee."[7] The collection was significantly increased by the artworks and objects sent to the president by Meriwether Lewis and William Clark during their western voyage.

The amalgamation of disparate objects mirrors the relentless curiosity of their owner and is the fundamental characteristic of Jefferson's collecting, which went hand in hand with his desire to educate and advance the citizens of his country. Nowhere in the United States, at that time, would anyone have been able to see such a mingling of objects. In a country today known more than any other for its encyclopedic museums, one of the earliest was that created by Thomas Jefferson at Monticello. In April 1782, the Marquis de Chastellux visited Jefferson and aptly observed: "At other times, natural philosophy was the subject of our conversations, and at still others, politics or the arts, for no object has escaped Mr. Jefferson; and it seems indeed as though, ever since his youth, he had placed his mind, like his house, on a lofty height, whence he might contemplate the whole universe."[8]

1   Jefferson to John Adams, August 15, 1820, in *The Papers of Thomas Jefferson: Retirement Series*, ed. J. Jefferson Looney (Princeton, NJ: Princeton University Press, 2004–), 16:195. Hereafter cited as *PTJ:RS*.

2   In preparing this essay, I am indebted to Diane Ehrenpreis, Monticello's Associate Curator, for her guidance and generosity with her recent research; and to Susan Stein, Richard Gilder Senior Curator, for her groundbreaking book, *The Worlds of Thomas Jefferson at Monticello* (1993), and her continuing research on Jefferson and the arts in America.

3   Thomas Jefferson to James Madison, September 20, 1785, in *The Papers of Thomas Jefferson*, ed. Julian P. Boyd (vols. 1–20), Barbara B. Oberg (vols. 29–41), and others (Princeton, NJ: Princeton University Press, 1950–), 8:535. Hereafter cited as *PTJ*.

4   Benjamin Henry Latrobe to Thomas Jefferson, August 13, 1807, Thomas Jefferson Papers, Library of Congress, Washington, D.C.

5   Thomas Jefferson to John Trumbull, February 15, 1789, in *PTJ*, 14:561.

6   George Ticknor, "Account of a Visit to Monticello," [February 4–7, 1815], in *PTJ:RS*, 8:238.

7   Thomas Jefferson, "Catalogue of Paintings at Monticello," [ca. 1809–15], in Susan Stein, *The Worlds of Thomas Jefferson at Monticello* (New York: Harry N. Abrams, in association with the Thomas Jefferson Memorial Foundation, 1993), 434.

8   Marquis de Chastellux, *Travels in North America in the Years 1780, 1781, and 1782*, trans. Howard C. Rice, Jr. (Chapel Hill: University of North Carolina Press, 1963), 392.

OPPOSITE
In the Hall, Jefferson displayed ancient and contemporary art from Europe and America, including his copy of Sleeping Ariadne, after the ancient Roman interpretation of the Hellenistic original.

PARLOR

PAGE 93
Jefferson installed an eclectic mix of French and American furnishings in the Parlor. The intricate French-style beech-and-cherry parquet floor was among the most sophisticated of any in the United States.

PAGES 94–95
Semi-octagonal in plan and two stories in height, the Parlor expresses the French and Roman neoclassicism that Jefferson admired while living in Europe.

PAGES 96–97
After Jefferson returned to the United States in 1789, he arranged to ship eighty-six crates of furnishings and art from Paris. These items—including the overmantel mirror, wall sconces, clock, and Sèvres porcelain figures centering the north wall of the Parlor—were eventually installed at Monticello.

PAGE 98
Certain scientific apparatus, like this air pump, were occasionally placed in the Parlor both to edify and entertain guests.

PAGE 99
Jefferson's miniature portrait by John Trumbull conveys a sense of liveliness and intimacy. Trumbull's portrait of Thomas Paine, below, was described by Jefferson as a "perfect likeness."

PAGES 100–101
Status symbols by virtue of their remarkable size, the Parlor pier mirrors have survived in place, undamaged and unaltered, for more than two hundred years.

PAGES 102–103
A Jefferson-era instrument, similar to the original, fills a space in the Parlor where an "Old Harpsichord" is identified on an 1826 plan of Monticello. Along with this book of music, Jefferson's harpsichord was used by generations of players.

OPPOSITE
Family and guests played chess and cards, particularly whist. Jefferson owned a 1746 edition of Edward Hoyle's *A Short Treatise on the Game of Whist*.

UPPER FLOORS

PAGE 107
The narrow north stairwell, and its southern counterpart, functioned as light and ventilation shafts, siphoning cool air from the cellars and focusing light from the skylights above.

PAGE 108
A black-framed mirror over a dressing table is typical of the simple furnishings in the upstairs bedrooms.

PAGE 109
After her widowhood in 1811, Jefferson's sister Anna Scott Jefferson Marks occupied this bedroom and installed her own furniture and bed hangings.

PAGES 110–111
When she returned as an adult to manage her father's household, Martha Jefferson Randolph lived in this second-story bedroom, where she installed this high chest acquired from friends and the French bedstead her father bought for her in Paris. The room is situated over Jefferson's library.

PAGE 112
All of the bed linens at Monticello were monogrammed and numbered in red thread, essential for inventory purposes. This pillowcase bears the initials of Martha Jefferson Randolph.

PAGE 113
Intended to protect the large hairstyles of the late eighteenth century, this bow-shaped calash may have been worn by Martha Wayles Skelton Jefferson or one of her daughters.

PAGE 114
An 1809 visitor to Monticello left one of few surviving descriptions of the Dome Room, which she called the most beautiful space in the house, even though it was unfurnished.

PAGE 115
Jefferson's granddaughters claimed a tiny attic space off the Dome Room as a secluded retreat to read or write letters—a counterpart to their grandfather's Cabinet.

PAGE 116–117
The Mars-yellow walls and grass-green floor of the Dome Room set off the large-scale base molding and cornice, which Jefferson derived from details of the Courtyard of the Temple of Nerva Trajan in Rome, as published in Andrea Palladio's *The Four Books of Architecture*.

OPPOSITE
Light fills the Dome Room through six large circular windows, as well as the oculus at the center of the dome.

WINE

AN APPRECIATION OF
THE GRAPE

Jay McInerney

In addition to being an architect, archaeologist, astronomer, jurist, musician, natural philosopher, slaveholder, statesman, author of the Declaration of Independence, and third president of the United States, Thomas Jefferson was the country's first wine geek. Most of the founding fathers were deeply fond of good claret and Madeira, but none were as passionate or systematic in their appreciation of the grape as Jefferson, who was utterly compulsive on the subject.

Both a connoisseur and a proselytizer, he planted dozens of grape varieties at Monticello and predicted that, someday, America would compete with France and Italy as a wine-producing nation. Believing that wine was much healthier than the whiskey and brandy that was being consumed in such vast quantities in our young republic, he pushed for lower import duties. "No nation is drunken where wine is cheap," he declared, "and none sober where the dearness of wine substitutes ardent spirits as the common beverage. It is in truth the only antidote to the bane of whisky."[1]

In 1784 as trade commissioner, Jefferson joined Benjamin Franklin and John Adams in Paris, fulfilling a long-held dream to spend time in Europe. He remained five years, succeeding Franklin as minister to France in 1785. Though his interest in wine seems to have developed during his student days at the College of William & Mary, it was only after the American Revolution, when he went to France, that his oenophilia really metastasized, according to John Hailman's authoritative 2006 study, *Thomas Jefferson on Wine*. Prior to that Jefferson seems, like most Americans, to have enjoyed Madeira and port, the fortified wines of Portugal. Not only did

PAGE 120
The looking glass over the Dining Room sideboard provided a dramatic backdrop for the service of wine, as well as the rinsing and storing of precious glassware and decanters.

LEFT
Archaeologists found material evidence of Jefferson's oenophilia in these late eighteenth-century English wine vessels, the more decorative one engraved MADEIRA.

OPPOSITE
The Wine Cellar was the most fortified room in Monticello, with bars on its window and this iron-reinforced door.

their higher alcohol content protect their character during the Atlantic crossing, they also were exempt from the British government's restrictions on French imports. Among the many liberties unleashed by the Revolution was the freedom to enjoy French wine.

"The first Thing to be done, in Paris," Adams wrote, "is always to send for a Taylor, a Peruke maker and Shoemaker, for this nation has established such a domination over the Fashion that neither Cloaths, Wigs nor Shoes made in any other Place will do in Paris."[2] Jefferson seems to have followed this advice; Mather Brown's portrait of him, painted in Paris in 1786, shows him looking fairly dandy in a powdered wig. Practically the next thing he did was to order twelve cases of Haut-Brion, the great first-growth Bordeaux, which was the first brand-name wine to appear in English literature:

Samuel Pepys had mentioned it as having "a most perticular taste,"[3] and it was subsequently one of only four estates to be ranked as first growths in the classification of 1855.

In 1787, after succeeding the ailing Franklin as American minister to France, Jefferson made a trip through France and Italy that he described to Lafayette as "combining public service with private gratification."[4] Officially he was checking out prospects for American trade, but his itinerary took him through most of the great wine regions of Europe, starting in Burgundy and moving on to the Rhône Valley, making his way down into Italy's Piedmont before looping north again to Bordeaux. Most of Jefferson's widely quoted writing about wine comes from his journal of this journey and a subsequent one to Germany's Rhine and Mosel regions,

as well as to Champagne. He was a keen observer. While in Burgundy he notes that in Volnay they eat "good wheat bread" whereas in nearby Meursault, it's rye. "I asked the reason of the difference. They told me that the white wines fail in quality much oftener than the red . . . the farmer therefore cannot afford to feed his labourers so well."[5]

Much of what Jefferson wrote about the character of the countries and wines he encountered could have been written last week, spelling eccentricities aside. "Chambertin, Voujeau and Veaune are strongest,"[6] he says of the red wines of Burgundy's Côte de Nuits; he declares "Diquem" (Château d'Yquem) the best Sauternes—observations that wouldn't seem terribly out of place in the current issue of *Wine Spectator*.

It's hard to imagine any aspect of contemporary life that Jefferson would recognize if he were suddenly to reappear among us, with one exception: he would be very comfortable navigating the wine list of a three-star restaurant in Paris. It is partly a testament to his connoisseurship and partly to the durability and conservatism of European wine traditions that many of the wines Jefferson drank and collected are the same ones that excite the interest of today's grape nuts. Almost a century before the official classification of the great growths of Bordeaux, Jefferson recorded a hierarchy remarkably similar to the present classification. In addition to Haut-Brion he ordered multiple cases of Lafite, Margaux, and Château d'Yquem for the cellar of his new residence, the Hôtel de Langeac on the Champs-Élysées. All of these wines sit at the top of the 1855 classification. He also sent many of these wines to President George Washington, who was happy to be the beneficiary of Jefferson's increasing expertise. When Jefferson occupied the President's House himself, he raised the standard of hospitality considerably, spending lavishly on food and wine—one factor in his later bankruptcy. Afterward, at Monticello, he became a budget drinker, substituting the wines of southern France and Tuscany for the great growths of Bordeaux and Burgundy. And he continued having vines planted, hoping that Monticello might someday produce wines to rival those of the Old World. In this quest he would turn out to be just a couple centuries ahead of his time.

Jefferson is usually assumed to be a Bordeaux man, because he wrote the most about it and perhaps because it seems like the wine that best reflects his character; claret, as the English call it, is an Apollonian wine, a beverage for intellectuals, for men of patience and reason. Austere in its youth, it predictably develops great complexity over the years. There are few surprises in Bordeaux. Burgundy, on the other hand, engages the emotions more than the intellect—a wine for the lunatic, the lover, and the poet. So it comes as a bit of a shock to learn from Hailman's book that during his years in Paris, when he had access to all the great growths of France, the sober sage of Monticello stocked his cellar with more Burgundy than Bordeaux, and his taste in them seems to have been impeccable: he was partial to the reds of Volnay, still a connoisseur's wine; among the whites, he liked Montrachet, which remains the most coveted white wine on the planet, though he sometimes chose the less expensive Meursault "Goutte d'Or," a robust white Burgundy from a slightly less exalted slope just down the road. Perhaps Jefferson's apparent preference for Burgundy while in Paris will eventually lead to one of those reassessments of his character, which seem to arrive every decade or two.

1   Thomas Jefferson to Jean Guillaume Hyde de Neuville, December 13, 1818, in *The Papers of Thomas Jefferson: Retirement Series*, ed. J. Jefferson Looney (Princeton, NJ: Princeton University Press, 2004–), 13:489–90.

2   John Adams, diary entry, October 26, 1782, in *Diary and Autobiography of John Adams*, ed. L. H. Butterfield (Cambridge, MA: Belknap Press of Harvard University Press, 1961), 3:37.

3   Samuel Pepys, diary entry, April 10, 1663, in *The Diary of Samuel Pepys*, ed. Robert Latham and William Matthews (London: HarperCollins, 1995), 4:100.

4   Thomas Jefferson to Lafayette, August 4, 1781, in *The Papers of Thomas Jefferson*, ed. Julian P. Boyd (vols. 1–20), Barbara B. Oberg (vols. 29–41), and others (Princeton, NJ: Princeton University Press, 1950–), 6:112. Hereafter cited as *PTJ*.

5   Thomas Jefferson, "Notes of a Tour into the Southern Parts of France, &c.," March 3–June 10, 1787, in *PTJ*, 11:417.

6   Ibid.

OPPOSITE
Jefferson planted his experimental vineyards below the Vegetable Garden retaining wall, where the south sun and mountain breeze would discourage both disease and insects.

IN GOOD TASTE AND ABUNDANCE

Alice Waters

"First patch of peas come to table," Thomas Jefferson wrote on May 22, 1773, in his "Garden Book," meticulously kept for nearly sixty years. "Note this spring is remarkably forward."[1] When we talk of Thomas Jefferson's cuisine—the foods he served, loved, and brought into the consciousness of the young nation he helped to found—we are also talking of Thomas Jefferson's garden. It is impossible to separate the two. Jefferson ate what we might now describe as a very modern twenty-first-century plant-based diet: "I have lived temperately," Jefferson wrote at age seventy-five, "eating little animal food, & that, not as an aliment so much as a condiment for the vegetables, which constitute my principal diet."[2] And why wouldn't his diet be mostly vegetables, when he grew such a rich diversity at his doorstep? Take, for example, Jefferson's beloved peas: he likely cultivated at least fifteen varieties at Monticello, in staggered plantings, so he would be able to eat them fresh from May through July. (Indeed, Jefferson maintained a friendly competition among his neighbors to see who could grow and harvest the earliest batch of peas of the year.) Year after year, that first appearance of the peas at the dinner table is lovingly documented. One year, it is May 31; another, May 18. In 1814, we know the day the peas first sprouted, the day they first flowered, and the day the first pod appeared. By 1819, Jefferson's garden yielded a new variety of early pea, which he called "May peas,"[3] that came to table by May 13. As you read through these careful notations, you can feel Jefferson's patient, joyful accrual of agricultural knowledge over the course of his whole life.

PAGE 126
With its elevated, southeast-facing site, the Vegetable Garden enjoys a favorable microclimate for early- and late-season plantings.

LEFT
Jefferson cultivated more than three hundred varieties of vegetables and herbs in his one-thousand-foot-long experimental garden, including one of his early-to-late-season mainstays, peas.

OPPOSITE
Globe, or French, artichokes were first cultivated in the Vegetable Garden in 1770.

The thousand-foot-long garden terrace carved into Monticello's mountainside was a horticultural lab maintained by enslaved laborers, and the fruits of Jefferson's diligent research were displayed every day in the Dining Room. Jefferson's curiosity for new and undiscovered food varietals extended far beyond peas: the garden was home to forty-four varieties of beans, thirty varieties of cabbage, and rice varietals retrieved from all over the world. The abundance of biodiversity goes on: asparagus, rhubarb, artichoke, Tuscan kale, French sorrel, tiny hot peppers from present-day Texas, West Indian gherkin cucumbers, mâche lettuce, olive trees, and tomatoes. The enslaved gardeners at Monticello produced a remarkable quantity of produce, in both scale and variety. The principal gardener in Jefferson's later years, Wormley Hughes, began his training in botany at the age of thirteen and spent his life working in the soil of central Virginia. Jefferson was a devoted seed saver, championing and distributing his latest vegetable and fruit discoveries to family, politicians, and neighbors alike so that they, too, could expand and awaken their tastes. There were around 130 enslaved people living at Monticello at any given time, and they brought with them their own knowledge of plants and important food traditions from Africa. They influenced the introduction of new ingredients such as okra, sesame plants, and sweet potatoes, which were welcomed into the garden and kitchen of Monticello, and sometimes even purchased directly from the enslaved families out of their personal gardens.

Jefferson's food curiosity was ever expanding. In 1784, he traveled to Paris for the first time (he would become the American minister to France in 1785) and fell in love with French arts and culture—and, of course, its food. Jefferson brought his enslaved manservant James Hemings with him to receive schooling in French culinary arts, and by the time Jefferson and Hemings returned to America several years later, they brought back new and revolutionary ideas about French and European foods and the equipment necessary to accomplish them. After eating at Monticello, American statesman Daniel Webster remarked in 1824 that the food at Jefferson's table was served in "half Virginian, half French style, in good taste & abundance."[4] You might find European novelties such as ice cream, *blanc-manger*, "maccaroni" noodles, and *pommes frites* at the table alongside a West African–influenced okra gumbo with rice, mashed potatoes, the freshest salad greens from the garden, and a plate of ripe nutmeg melons. These meals had an informal feeling, with dinner

OPPOSITE
Jefferson sited log dwellings above the garden along Mulberry Row. Each building, two hundred square feet or less, had a loft over the ground floor so as to house an entire enslaved family in two rooms.

guests who ranged from politicians and travelers from abroad to clergymen, doctors, botanists, and extended family members. Diners served themselves, thanks to several ingenious dumbwaiters (including a hidden wine dumbwaiter), and were seated "pell-mell" (informally) and not according to rank; I believe Jefferson did this because he understood the democratizing power of gathering around the table, sharing food, and exchanging knowledge. These meals were Jefferson's way of feeding people ideas.

While the cooks of Monticello were certainly capable of putting together a grand repast for the many visitors who crossed the threshold, there was still a simplicity that underscored Jefferson's cuisine, always defined by what was ripe and in season, or preserved for winter use. The truth is, when you have food that is as fresh and ripe and vibrant as his was—with that sort of breathtaking biodiversity at your fingertips—you don't need to do very much to it. Jefferson's kitchen isn't very big, and it seems deceptively spare: a big open cooking hearth, a rotisserie, copper pots, iron cooking utensils.

OPPOSITE
Several varieties of tomatoes, which Jefferson referred to as "tomatas," were planted yearly between 1809 and 1824.

BELOW
When Jefferson expanded the house, he ordered this larger second kitchen constructed, which featured the most progressive technology and sophisticated cookware of any in America. Completed in 1809, it included a large cooking hearth with a rotisserie and bake oven.

Several years ago, I had the good fortune of being able to cook in that kitchen with my friend Scott Peacock, a Southern cook and cookbook author; I spent the morning picking lettuces in the gardens, then attempted to milk a dairy cow named Triticale, and churned her milk into butter for biscuits, which Scott then cooked over that open hearth. I like to think of myself as someone who eats locally and in rhythm with the seasons, but it struck me in that moment that my way of living is nothing compared to the way that Jefferson lived his life: profoundly and intimately connected to the land that surrounded him and the food that came from it. Buried in the rich earth of Monticello are the roots of our democracy, founded on a deep respect for nature and the agrarian values of our forebears. All we need to do is dig those values up again.

1   Thomas Jefferson, *Thomas Jefferson's Garden Book, 1766–1824, with Relevant Extracts from His Other Writings*, ed. Edwin Morris Betts (Charlottesville, VA: Thomas Jefferson Memorial Foundation, 1999), 40.

2   Thomas Jefferson to Vine Utley, March 21, 1819, in *The Papers of Thomas Jefferson: Retirement Series*, ed. J. Jefferson Looney (Princeton, NJ: Princeton University Press, 2004–), 14:156.

3   Jefferson, *Garden Book*, 582.

4   Daniel Webster, "Notes of Mr. Jefferson's Conversation 1824 at Monticello," in *The Papers of Daniel Webster, Series 1: Correspondence*, ed. Charles M. Wiltse (Hanover, NH: Published for Dartmouth College by the University Press of New England, 1974), 1:371.

OPPOSITE
Included in the eighty-six crates of wares that Jefferson had shipped from Paris in 1790 was a full complement of French copper cookware. Each burner of the state-of-the-art eight-burner stew stove (copper pieces are resting on two of the burners here) could be warmed by coals to a different temperature.

DINING ROOM

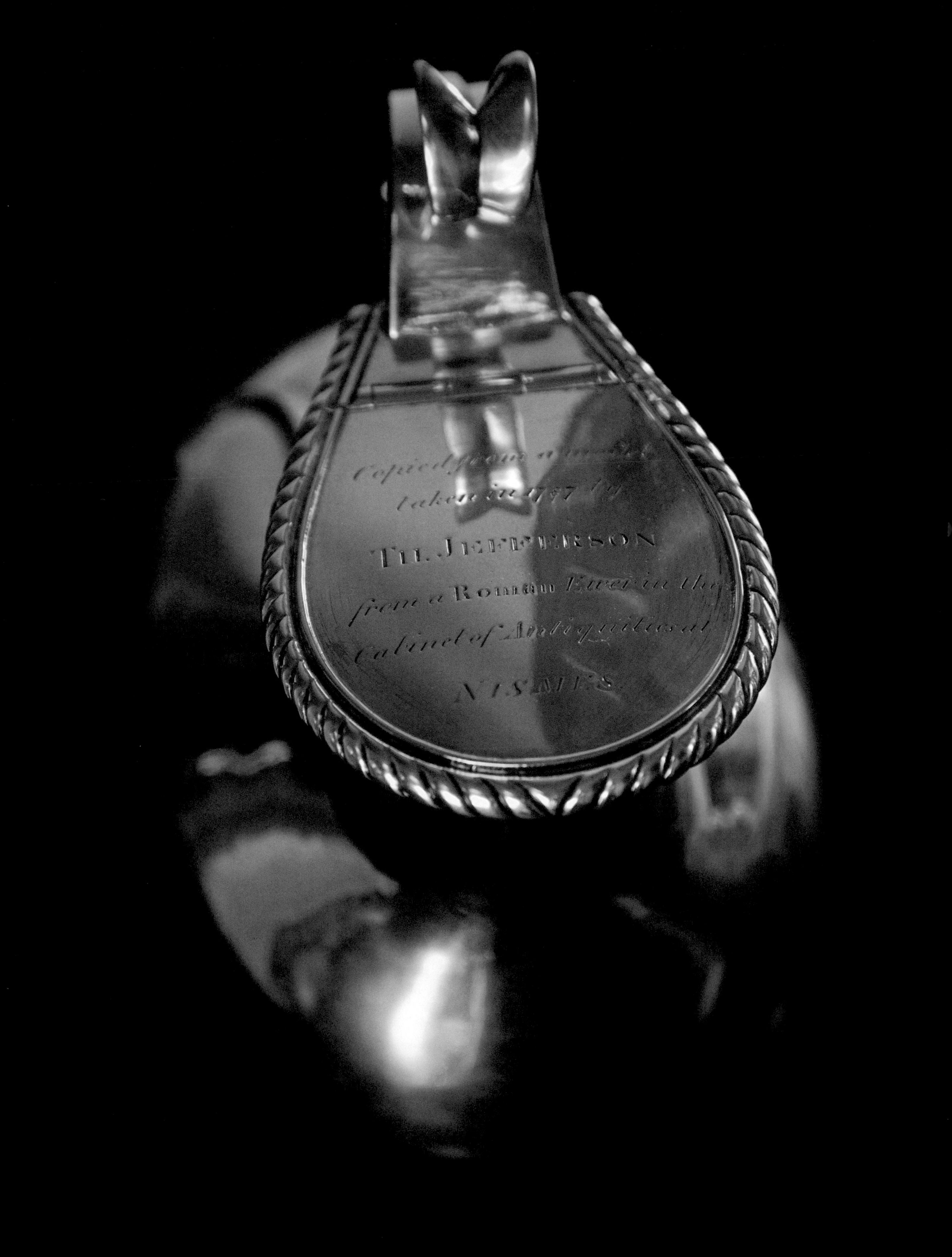
TH. JEFFERSON
from a Roman Ewer in the
NISMES

TEA ROOM

PAGE 149
Jefferson used this diminutive and fashionably neoclassical French silver urn, purchased in Paris in 1789, as a coffee pot.

PAGES 150–151
The Tea Room was an intimate and elegant sitting room where family and visitors read, conversed, painted, courted, and took refreshment.

PAGE 152
Archaeological evidence confirms that green-edged tableware imported from England was widely used at Monticello.

PAGE 153
Martha Wayles Skelton Jefferson brought this English silver ladle to her new home when she married Thomas Jefferson in 1772.

OPPOSITE
A patinated plaster bust of Benjamin Franklin, after Houdon's original, presides over the Tea Room, part of Jefferson's "most honorable suite."

AS FAR AS THE EYE
COULD SEE

Thomas Jefferson's composition of farm, forest, gardens, and grounds at Monticello stands as an extraordinary example of comprehensive landscape design, perhaps the first of its scale and complexity in American history. Originally a 5,000-acre plantation (of which 2,600 acres remain generally intact), the composition emerged from the European concept of *ferme ornée*, or ornamental farm, which combined productive agriculture, enhancement of the natural context, bold reshaping of existing topographic features, and expansive collections of both native and non-native plants for pleasure and production. For his buildings and landscapes at Monticello, Jefferson drew directly from ancient, Renaissance, and Enlightenment design concepts. The landscape design evolved in tandem with his vision for democracy and pluralism in the society of ideas that he was striving to

create. The social experiment of American democracy relied upon the design of structures that created an orderly balance between the natural impulses of humankind and the regulations of collective self-governance. In Jefferson's comprehensive vision for Monticello, we find a similar balance between the expressive forces of nature and the discipline of landscape design.

Jefferson began planning and shaping this landscape after he took possession of his inheritance upon reaching majority at age twenty-one. But he had been thinking about its design much earlier. As a boy he had roamed the hill overlooking his family home and vowed to someday build his house atop it. He later named his new home and the entire plantation for this defining feature: Monticello, Italian for "little mountain." The siting of his house on a mountaintop greatly increased

PAGE 156
Jefferson installed his weather vane atop the roof of the Northeast Portico and connected it to a compass rose directly below on the portico's ceiling, so he could easily monitor wind direction with a glance through the glass doors of his entry hall.

LEFT
The winding-walk flower border, which Jefferson sketched in a letter to his granddaughter Anne Cary Randolph, was laid out in the spring of 1808.

OPPOSITE
Jefferson situated the South Orchard, or Fruitery, just below the Vegetable Garden wall; it contained more than one thousand fruit trees, including one hundred sixty peach trees. In 1815 Jefferson wrote, "We abound in the luxury of the peach."

the difficulty of construction and ongoing provisioning, while reducing access to water. In perhaps his boldest design stroke, Jefferson ordered the crown of the mountain sliced away; tons of earth were displaced by enslaved laborers working with the aid of animals. As Andrea Wulf has noted: "Instead of rich yields and easy access to Richmond and Fredericksburg, Jefferson had chosen glorious views over the seemingly endless lines of the Blue Ridge Mountains that stood as the western signposts for the wilderness beyond."[1] The nearly three-acre plateau created on the top of the mountain became the canvas upon which Jefferson would situate the roads, orchards, terraces, and gardens, both ornamental and productive, that would form the framework of his landscape design.

Jefferson's desire to situate his home atop an elongated, conical landform harked to his boyhood vision, but it also reveals the influence of the siting theory of the Italian Renaissance villa. This is evident in Jefferson's reliance on internal ordering axes, connections to symbolic external prospects, and considerations of air flow and solar aspect. Jefferson's foremost inspiration in this regard was Andrea Palladio. Jefferson pronounced his writings "the Bible"[2] and owned several copies of Palladio's *Four Books of Architecture*. In book 2, chapter XII, Palladio addresses the location of villas: "Let a place be chosen . . . in the middle of the estate, that the owner, without much trouble, may view and improve it on every side."[3] From his little mountain, Jefferson enjoyed expansive views of his agricultural holdings. Palladio describes the design of the private villa and its surrounding landscape as an agricultural enterprise of production and income, not solely a retreat for pleasure. Jefferson ingeniously integrated elements of agricultural production, landscape, and architecture, as revealed in his layout of Monticello's dependencies, passageways, stables, gardens, and kitchens. Palladio continues, "And, finally, in the choice of the situation for the building of a villa, all those considerations ought to be had, which are necessary in a city house; since the

city is as it were but a great house, and, on the contrary, a country house is a little city."[4]

Monticello's grounds and gardens have been the subject of scholarship and study for generations, but one theory seems of particular relevance in exploring the comprehensive design mind of Jefferson vis-à-vis his landscape vision—the inherent political symbolism. Wulf has explored the political statement made explicit at the founding fathers' private estates through their reliance on plants native to North America in the flower gardens, borders, and arboreal collections. Jefferson as well as James Madison, John Adams, and George Washington were in regular dialogue about the symbolism of these plants and the intentional political narrative their use embodied by representing the new nation. As Wulf writes, "The garden that Jefferson designed at Monticello during his last years of the presidency combined his appreciation for beauty and his love for his country with his scientific and agricultural endeavors—it was a celebration of the United States of America and the future."[5]

Jefferson not only celebrated the nation but also devoted himself to improving it, not just in politics but in many diverse disciplines, including horticulture. His relentless curiosity and abiding belief in innovation drove him to search out or send for plants and cultivars in Europe and Asia. "The greatest service which can be rendered any country is to add an useful plant to its culture," Jefferson wrote.[6] Peter Hatch, Monticello's emeritus director of gardens and grounds, has eloquently called the estate's vegetable garden "an Ellis Island of introduced economic plants, some 330 varieties of ninety-nine species of vegetables and herbs."[7]

Such a garden required an equally bold ordering of the productive landscape. Jefferson placed his thousand-foot-long vegetable terrace on the flank of the mountain south of the house and dependencies. As with nearly all construction at Monticello, the garden represents Herculean effort by the enslaved laborers, who carved out the hillside and constructed the massive retaining wall as high as twelve feet in places. The garden's sheer scale, as Wulf has remarked, made Jefferson "the most extraordinary gardener in the United States."[8] Its siting also endowed it with stunning views, thereby uniting utility and beauty, a cornerstone of Jefferson's *ferme ornée* vision. To that end, he sited orchards and vineyards just below the retaining wall. Not only did they benefit from the drying morning sun and continual air flow along the slopes (thus reducing mold and rot in the humid climate of central Virginia), they also improved the aesthetic composition, displacing native forest that obscured the majestic views and disrupted Jefferson's ability to survey from the mountaintop the majority of his plantation below. Today the dramatic views remain, but of the forests that have supplanted the plantation fields.

The vegetable garden was a vast and extraordinary laboratory of production surrounded by a ten-foot-tall paling fence with a locked gate to prevent theft by people or animals. As Hatch has explained, Jefferson based his garden plan on the tenets described by Bernard McMahon, the Philadelphia horticulturalist and nurseryman whose 1806 publication, *The American Gardener's Calendar*, initiated an eight-year correspondence with Jefferson. Yet Jefferson added such innovations as circular terraces and submural beds,

which were narrow "forcing beds" located near the warmth of the garden wall. Hatch goes on to note, "Jefferson used unique plant combinations for the borders he documented in the Monticello vegetable garden. In 1813 he noted planting okra as an 'edging' to square X, which was planted with tomatoes, while the carrot square XIII was bordered by sesame."[9] Jefferson's deep understanding of horticulture may not have been remarkable for his era, but when combined with his (self-trained) understanding of earthworks, grading, drainage, surveying, and complex site construction, he again stands out as unique for his time.

Perhaps one of the most sophisticated examples of Jefferson's comprehensive landscape design was the network of carriage roads that artfully circumnavigates the irregular topographic features of the mountain at

LEFT
The East Road follows the ridgeline up the mountain from the floodplain along the river. Once flanked by fields and woodlands, today it is completely shaded in forest.

OPPOSITE
The site of the ford across the Rivanna River, which bisected Jefferson's plantation at the foot of Monticello Mountain. Shadwell, the farm where Jefferson was born, is on the left bank of the river.

relatively consistent elevations, forming a complex system for pleasure and utility. Jefferson observed and sketched a similar network in the Odenwald mountains near Heidelberg in southwest Germany, and brought the idea home.[10] He called them "roundabouts" and connected them to one another with diagonal roads that, for scenic rides, rose only one foot for every twenty feet of distance and, for utilitarian purposes, rose one in every ten. This network of arcs and crossroads brings a frame of order to the mountain, achieving a constant gradient that eased the burden on horses and oxen while revealing the landscape through gradually opening sweeps of forest and long views of farmland and mountains.

One particular landscape revealed on a roundabout nearing the house exemplifies Jefferson's appreciation of the fecundity of the native Piedmont Virginia forest and his desire to adapt that ecology to resemble English landscape gardens he had visited. Just northwest of the pleasure gardens adjoining the house, he created The Grove. As he described it, "Let your ground be covered with trees of the loftiest stature. Trim up their bodies as high as the constitution & form of the tree will bear, but so as that their tops shall still unite and yield a dense shade. A wood, so open below, will have nearly the appearance of open grounds."[11] This shady retreat could then operate as a canvas onto which drifts of flowering shrubs could be introduced. The Grove also satisfied a need uncommon in England. Under "the beaming, constant & almost vertical sun of Virg[ini]a," Jefferson remarked, "shade is our Elysium."[12]

In contrast to the elliptical geometries of the roundabouts, the East Road and Mulberry Row stand as two interesting exceptions that provide internal ordering axes in the Italian Renaissance tradition. The East Road was a preexisting ridgeline route that provided access to the agricultural fields. Once Jefferson placed his house at the lofty terminus of the road, it became his principal arrival route and marked the connection, both literal and symbolic, to Richmond, the state capital.

The East Road began at Shadwell, Jefferson's birthplace, forded the Rivanna River, and slowly rose from the floodplain up the ridge of the mountain through the fields. By the 1790s, these swidden-cleared fields were fixed in place and largely converted from hand-managed tobacco cultivation to plow-cultivated grain crops. As the road emerged from the fields and approached the house, Jefferson flanked it to the north with an orchard, more evidence of his *ferme ornée* design philosophy.

By 1806 Jefferson had ordered surveys and begun construction for an alternative entry route, one that did not bisect the topography but followed its contours and created a sequence of idyllic views: of river and forest, productive and pastoral fields, as well as rocky outcroppings and other natural features of the mountain ridge. "Jefferson had carefully staged these different elements of his garden, turning the changing landscape along the winding roads that led up the mountain to the mansion into an orchestrated approach," as Wulf has written. "In some places roads were cut into the slope, while in others large areas were raised or flattened; fields were carved out of the forest, and elsewhere trees were planted to create groves. The closer to the house, the more controlled the landscape became, almost like a journey from wilderness to civilisation."[13] Jefferson's new entry, known as the North Road, epitomized this approach; traversing both natural and productive landscapes, it artfully communicated the compositional intent of the mind that envisioned it, as if Jefferson were narrating the journey. Soon after the road's completion, Jefferson wrote to Madison and recommended that he use it on his next visit.[14]

In contrast to winding carriage roads, Mulberry Row was a straight dirt lane that ran above and parallel to the garden quite close to the house, its linearity at odds with the arcing topography of the mountain and visually reinforced by the intervention of the vegetable terrace's stone retaining wall. A flanking allée of mulberry trees added order to the composition while providing shade for the dwellings of enslaved people and the workshops that constituted Monticello's industrial hub—the nailery, storehouse for iron, coal sheds, joinery, carpenter shop, saw pit, and textile workshop.

Mulberry Row ends on the brow of the mountain, revealing the same vista Jefferson had created for his residence, one that featured Montalto, the higher mountain to the south. Tellingly, Montalto was one of Jefferson's first land purchases, secured in 1771, and it followed the massive earthworks project that leveled and cleared the home site. Indeed, it was that project that

first revealed Montalto, Italian for "high mountain," as the ideal "symbolic external prospect" cited in the treatises of Italian Renaissance landscape design. Jefferson approached his neighbor in 1771 to "give me as much of his nearest mountain as can be seen from mine, and 100 yds. beyond the line of sight."[15] Thus the parallel axes of the house—Mulberry Row and the garden—align with the spine of the mountain and focus on Montalto, while being encircled and balanced by the meandering, discovery sequence of roundabouts.

At Monticello, Jefferson, with no formal training, pioneered and demonstrated mastery of the full skillset that underlies the modern-day profession of landscape architecture. He integrated the various natural features and agricultural functions of his landscape into a comprehensive design, at the time unprecedented in the United States for its scale or drama. The artful entry sequence of river, forests, fields, and orchards, amplified with encircling carriage roads, crescendos to reveal the stunning views of a mountaintop villa and its gardens. He could justly be regarded as the nation's first modern landscape architect, designing all that the eye could see.

1   Andrea Wulf, *Founding Gardeners: How the Revolutionary Generation Created an American Eden* (London: William Heinemann, 2011), 42–43.

2   Isaac A. Coles, "Account of a Conversation with Thomas Jefferson," [before February 23, 1816], in *The Papers of Thomas Jefferson: Retirement Series*, ed. J. Jefferson Looney (Princeton, NJ: Princeton University Press, 2004–), 9:500.

3   Andrea Palladio, *The Four Books of Architecture* [1570] (New York: Dover Publications, 1965), 46.

4   Ibid., 47.

5   Wulf, *Founding Gardeners*, 197.

6   Thomas Jefferson, "Summary of Public Service," [after September 2, 1800], in *The Papers of Thomas Jefferson*, ed. Julian P. Boyd (vols. 1–20), Barbara B. Oberg (vols. 29–41), and others (Princeton, NJ: Princeton University Press, 1950–), 32:124. Hereafter cited as *PTJ*.

7   Peter J. Hatch, *A Rich Spot of Earth: Thomas Jefferson's Revolutionary Garden at Monticello* (New Haven, CT: Yale University Press, 2012), 4.

8   Wulf, *Founding Gardeners*, 206.

9   Hatch, *Rich Spot of Earth*, 79–80.

10 Thomas Jefferson, "Notes of a Tour through Holland and the Rhine Valley," March 3–April 23, 1788, in *PTJ*, 13:24. Jefferson erroneously recorded the site of this road network as the "Bergstrasse" mountains, in confusion with an ancient Roman road that runs through the region called the *Bergstrasse* (or "mountain road").

11 Thomas Jefferson to William Hamilton, July 31, 1806, Thomas Jefferson Papers, Library of Congress, Washington, D.C.

12 Ibid.

13 Wulf, *Founding Gardeners*, 199–200.

14 Thomas Jefferson to James Madison, September 2, 1806, James Madison Papers, Library of Congress, Washington, D.C.

15 Thomas Jefferson, memorandum, March 24, 1771, in *Jefferson's Memorandum Books. Accounts, with Legal Records and Miscellany, 1767–1826*, ed. James A. Bear Jr. and Lucia C. Stanton (Princeton, NJ: Princeton University Press, 1997), 219.

OPPOSITE
Montalto, as seen from the roof of the house, rises 410 feet above Monticello, with an elevation of 1,278 feet.

PAGES 168–169
Jefferson integrated the natural features of the land into the designs for his residence and landscape. He selected as a site the first mountains rising from the gently rolling Piedmont plain, viewed here stretching east toward the Atlantic coast.

GARDENS
MULBERRY ROW
LANDSCAPE

PAGE 171
With the backdrop of the Blue Ridge Mountains, Jefferson mounted his unusual spherical sundial atop a classical pedestal and a capital of Benjamin Henry Latrobe's "American" order of architecture, featuring tobacco or corn, the latter seen here.

PAGES 172–173
By cleverly submerging the wings that flanked the house under terraces, Jefferson preserved the grace and drama of his "essay in architecture," allowing it to preside without interruption on the flattened crown of the mountain.

PAGE 174
Late-summer annuals abound along the winding walk encircling the West Lawn. The borders were divided into ten-foot sections in 1812, each with a single variety of flower.

PAGE 175
Spider flower (*Cleome bassleriana*) was a popular, self-seeding annual in the flower gardens.

PAGE 176
Both ornamental and functional, the allée of Mulberry Row provided vital shade during hot Virginia summers.

PAGE 177
Based on Jefferson's writings and archaeological evidence, some of the cabins along Mulberry Row have been reconstructed, including this one, which may have been occupied by John and Priscilla Hemmings.

PAGE 178
Only the chimney remains of the joiner's shop on Mulberry Row, where John Hemmings would have crafted furniture for Monticello.

PAGE 179
On April 30, 1774, Jefferson noted that seed of "white beet from England" had been sown, referring to Swiss chard, an ancient European vegetable with ribbed foliage in mixed colors.

PAGES 180–181
Tons of earth were removed by enslaved laborers to create the one-thousand-foot-long terrace for the Vegetable Garden. At the midpoint, Jefferson centered his Garden Pavilion for reading and contemplation.

PAGE 182
In his Garden Book, Jefferson sporadically recorded the first artichokes to "come to table" and the "last dish" of them, from 1794 to 1825. If the edible "chokes" are left on the plant, they develop into purple, thistle-like flowers.

PAGE 183
A cross between a cantaloupe and a muskmelon, the Anne Arundel melon is documented in Maryland as early as 1731.

PAGES 184–185
Jefferson divided the garden into squares, such as this one that includes teepees of lima beans and rows of okra and corn.

PAGES 186–187
The Rivanna River was a critical feature for the plantation, providing water power for grist- and sawmills, and transportation of crops and goods, as well as serving as a scenic backdrop for walks and rides. But its floods were also a threat, repeatedly damaging mills and dams.

OPPOSITE
A May Duke cherry tree marks the southwest terminus of the Vegetable Garden.

CONCLUSION

ARCHITECT OF AMERICAN PROGRESS

*T*homas Jefferson loved his books, his house, his farms, good wine, architecture, Homer, horseback riding, history, France, the Commonwealth of Virginia, spending money, and his family. He believed in America, and in Americans. The nation, he said in his first inaugural address, in 1801, was "the world's best hope,"[1] a phrase that would be echoed by both Abraham Lincoln and Ronald Reagan. He thought Americans themselves capable of virtually anything they put their minds to. "Whatever they can," Jefferson remarked of his countrymen, "they will."[2]

The same might plausibly be said of Jefferson himself. In his devotion to the arts, to science, to reason, and to the republican experiment in liberty, he was a crucial architect of America. And the closest one can come to conversing with him is to come to Monticello, his beloved "little mountain"—a monument to curiosity and to the possibilities and the imperfections of human endeavor.

At Monticello, living was an art to be mastered, and no detail was too small to escape Jefferson's notice, whether political and philosophical or architectural and artistic. Meals were not only to sustain the body but also to feed the soul. Houses were not only to shield one from the elements but also to broaden the imagination. Paintings and sculpture were not only to fill space but also to shape one's sense of history and identity. Gardens were not only to produce flowers and fruits and vegetables but also to connect oneself inextricably to the natural world. The house, with its vast L-shaped terraces, Venetian porches, and piazzas, was designed to enable the enjoyment of the landscape. Monticello

served as a laboratory for Jefferson's cultivated life, a manifestation of his larger objective to educate friends and family as well as to live with "a greater eye to convenience."[3]

To his friends, who were numerous and devoted, Jefferson was among the greatest men who had ever lived, a renaissance figure who was formidable without seeming overbearing, sparkling without being showy, winning without appearing cloying. Yet to his foes, who were numerous and prolific, Jefferson was an atheist and a fanatic, a demagogue and a dreamer, a hypocrite who preached liberty but practiced slavery, a womanly Francophile who could not be trusted with the government of a great nation. His perennial task was to change those views as best he could. He longed for affection, for approval, for harmony.

He adored detail, noting the temperature each day and carrying a tiny, ivory-leaved notebook in his pocket to track his daily expenditures. He drove his horses hard and fast and considered the sun his "almighty physician."[4] Jefferson was fit and virile, a terrific horseman and inveterate walker. He drank no hard liquor but loved wine, taking three glasses a day and perhaps a bit more with a friend.

He possessed a genius for politics, philosophy, education; he was a vital maker of his nation's public, intellectual, and cultural lives. A master of emotional and political manipulation, sensitive to criticism, intoxicated by approval, obsessed with his reputation, devoted to America, he was irresistibly drawn to the great world, endlessly at work, as he put it, "to see the standard of reason at length erected, after so many ages during which the human mind has been held in vassalage by kings, priests, and nobles."[5] As a planter, lawyer, legislator, governor, diplomat, secretary of state, vice president, and president, Jefferson spent much of his life seeking control over himself and power over the lives and destinies of others.

He was shaped by the need to make the world conform to his will. He was the father of children (by his wife and by the enslaved Sally Hemings), of the ideal of individual liberty, of the Louisiana Purchase, of the Lewis and Clark expedition, of the American West. The father of the idea of American progress, of the animating national spirit that the future could be better than the present or the past, Jefferson has inspired the greatest of American politicians in ensuing generations who have prospered by projecting a Jeffersonian vision that the country's finest hours lie ahead.

PAGE 190
Monticello's Southwest Portico was a classical outdoor sitting room; today it is a dramatic setting for various events, including the annual naturalization ceremony on Independence Day.

PAGE 193
Jefferson's tall, slim riding boots correspond to his overseer's description of him: "Six feet two & a half inches high, well proportioned & straight as a gun-barrel. He was like a fine horse: he had no surplus flesh."

OPPOSITE
The leaves of Jefferson's ivory notebook could be wiped clean of slate-pencil markings and reused. A ghost of his notations is visible.

RIGHT
Jefferson acquired this polygraph machine in 1804 to make copies of his letters. Over his lifetime, he wrote nearly nineteen thousand letters; more than five thousand were written in the Cabinet at Monticello, after his retirement from public life in 1809.

Jefferson never tired of invention and inquiry, designing dumbwaiters and hidden mechanisms to open doors at Monticello. He delighted in archaeology, paleontology, astronomy, botany, and meteorology, and once created his own version of the Gospels. He drew sustenance from music, found joy in garden- ing, adored the arts of all kinds. He bought and built beautiful things, creating Palladian plans for Monticello and the Roman-inspired capitol of Virginia, which he designed after seeing the ruins of a temple in Nîmes, in the south of France. He was an enthusiastic patron of pasta, gave Americans the first recipe for ice cream, and enjoyed the search for the perfect dressing for his salads. He kept shepherd dogs (two favorites were named Bergère and Grizzle). He knew Latin, Greek, French, Italian, and Spanish.

A guest at a country inn was said to have once struck up a conversation with a "plainly-dressed and unassuming traveler" whom the stranger did not recognize. The two covered subject after subject, and the unremarkable traveler was "per- fectly acquainted with each." Afterward, "filled with wonder," the guest asked the landlord who this extraordinary man was. When the topic was the law, the traveler said, "he thought he was a lawyer"; when it was medicine, "he felt sure he was a physician"; when it was theology, "he became convinced that he was a clergyman."

The landlord's reply was brief. "Oh, why I thought you knew the Squire."[6]

Jefferson presented himself to the world as a philosopher and scientist, a naturalist and a historian—a man of the Enlightenment, always looking forward, consumed by the quest for knowledge and insight. And he was all these things.

Yet he was also an avid student of human nature, a keen observer of what drove other men. And he loved knowing the details of other lives. He admired the letters of Madame de Sévigné, whose huge correspondence offered a panoramic view of the France of Louis XIV, and Madame de Staël's *Corinne, or Italy*, a romantic picaresque novel that included the aphorism "To know all is to forgive all." In his library at Monticello was a collection of what a guest called "regal scandal"[7] that Jefferson had put together under the title "The Book of Kings." It included the *Mémoires de la Princesse de Bareith* (by the princess royal of Prussia, sister of Frederick the Great); *Les Mémoires de la Comtesse de la Motte* (by a key figure in a scandal involving a diamond necklace and Marie Antoinette); and an account of the trial of the Duke of York, the commander-in-chief of the British army who had been forced to resign amid charges that he had allowed his mistress to sell officer commissions. Jefferson pointed out these tales, his guest recalled, "with a satisfaction somewhat inconsistent with the measured gravity he claims in relation to such subjects generally."[8]

OPPOSITE
The North Terrace, off of the Tea Room, offers a stunning panorama of the Blue Ridge Mountains. Both the North and South Terraces cleverly disguised and sheltered the cellar-level wings so as to preserve views from the house.

RIGHT
After his return from France in 1789, Jefferson favored simpler clothing, such as this indigo-blue wool-and-cotton frock coat.

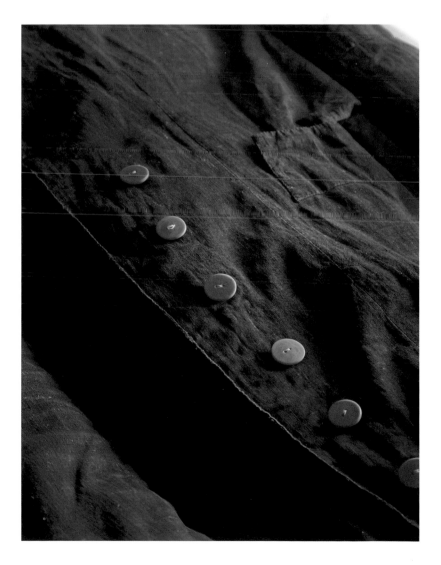

And the great world—or at least much of it—found him charming, brilliant, and gracious. Women in particular loved him. Calling on Samuel Harrison Smith, the Republican publisher of the Washington *National Intelligencer*, Jefferson was shown into the Smiths' parlor. There he spent a few minutes alone with Smith's wife, Margaret, a writer and hostess. The child of a Federalist family, Mrs. Smith did not at first realize who Jefferson was and found herself "somewhat checked by the dignified and reserved air" of the caller. What she experienced as a "chilled feeling," however, passed almost instantly. Offered a chair, the stranger assumed "a free and easy manner, and carelessly throwing his arm on the table near which he sat, he turned towards me a countenance beaming with an expression of benevolence and with a manner and voice almost femininely soft and gentle." Clearly gifted in the arts of the morning call, he "entered into conversation on the commonplace topics of the day," Mrs. Smith said, "from which, before I was conscious of it, he had drawn me into observations of a more personal and interesting nature."

Such was his charm that though she did not know quite why, here she was, saying things she had not meant to say. "There was something in his manner, his

countenance and voice that at once unlocked my heart." The caller was in a kind of control, reversing the usual order of things in which the host, not the hosted, set the terms and conditions of conversation. "I found myself frankly telling him what I liked or disliked in our present circumstances and abode," Mrs. Smith said. "I knew not who he was, but the interest with which he listened to my artless details . . . put me perfectly at my ease; in truth so kind and conciliating were his looks and manners that I forgot he was not a friend of my own."

At this point the door to the parlor opened, and Mr. Smith walked in. Learning that the caller was "*Mr. Jefferson*," Mrs. Smith was at once thrilled and embarrassed. "I felt my cheeks burn and my heart throb, and not a word more could I speak while he remained." She was struck by the gulf between the image and the man. "And is this the violent democrat, the vulgar demagogue, the bold atheist and profligate man I have so often heard denounced by the federalists?" she asked. "Can this man so meek and mild, yet dignified in his manners, with a voice so soft and low, with a countenance so benignant and intelligent, can he be that daring leader of a faction, that disturber of the peace, that enemy of all rank

OPPOSITE
A scientist of the Enlightenment, Jefferson observed and recorded the world around him, using a collection of scientific instruments he amassed over decades.

RIGHT
Jefferson designed his grave marker as a classical obelisk, with no mention of his presidency or positions—only the fruits of his ideas about government, religion, and education.

and order?" Taking his leave, Jefferson "shook hands cordially with us . . . and in a manner which said as plain as words could do, 'I am your friend.'"[9]

In his retirement at Monticello, he looked back over the years, through the haze of war and struggle and peril, and he felt that he had done his duty. "The circumstances of our country at my entrance into life," he remarked to a visitor, "were such that every honest man felt himself compelled to take a part, and to act up to the best of his abilities."[10] He could have done no other. The Revolution, Jefferson once said, had put everything at risk; it was a "bold and doubtful election . . . for our country, between submission, or the sword."[11]

Thomas Jefferson died at Monticello on July 4, 1826, the fiftieth anniversary of the Declaration of Independence. The three achievements he ordered carved on his tombstone at Monticello—as author of the Declaration of American Independence and of the Virginia Statute for Religious Freedom, and as founder of the University of Virginia—speak to his love of the liberty of the mind and of the heart, and to his faith in the future. They point toward the least disputable elements of his long, turbulent life, to the primacy of reason, the possibilities of freedom, and the eternal quest for wisdom. They point, too, to the making of things, to leadership. He fought for each of these causes and convinced enough of the world of the rightness of his vision that he left behind living monuments—and there is no greater monument than the nation itself, dedicated to the realization, however gradual and however painful, of the ideal amid the realities of a political world driven by ambition and selfishness.

For Jefferson never gave up on America, a country in many ways he brought into being and which he nurtured through tender, fragile hours. "And I have observed this march of civilization advancing from the sea coast, passing over us like a cloud of light, increasing our knolege and improving our condition," Jefferson wrote in 1824, ". . . and where this progress will stop no one can say."[12] Or so we hope still.

1   Thomas Jefferson, First Inaugural Address, March 4, 1801, in *The Papers of Thomas Jefferson*, ed. Julian P. Boyd (vols. 1–20), Barbara B. Oberg (vols. 29–41), and others (Princeton, NJ: Princeton University Press, 1950–), 33:149. Hereafter cited as *PTJ*.

2   Thomas Jefferson to James Monroe, October 16, 1814, in *The Papers of Thomas Jefferson: Retirement Series*, ed. J. Jefferson Looney (Princeton, NJ: Princeton University Press, 2004–), 8:32. Hereafter cited as *PTJ:RS*.

3   Thomas Jefferson to Mann Page, [May 16, 1796], in *PTJ*, 29:101.

4   Thomas Jefferson to James Monroe, March 18, 1785, in *PTJ*, 8:43.

5   Thomas Jefferson to James Madison, December 16, 1786, in *PTJ*, 10:604.

6   Sarah N. Randolph, *The Domestic Life of Thomas Jefferson* (New York: Harper & Brothers, 1871), 38.

7   George Ticknor, "Account of a Visit to Monticello," [February 4–7, 1815], in *PTJ:RS*, 8:240.

8   Ibid.

9   Margaret Bayard Smith, *The First Forty Years of Washington Society*, ed. Gaillard Hunt (New York: Charles Scribner's Sons, 1906), 5–8.

10   Ibid., 81.

11   Thomas Jefferson to Roger Chew Weightman, June 24, 1826, Thomas Jefferson Papers, Library of Congress, Washington, D.C.

12   Thomas Jefferson to William Ludlow, September 6, 1824, Thomas Jefferson Papers, Library of Congress, Washington, D.C.

OPPOSITE
Jefferson had only to step from his private suite onto the South Terrace to admire, in his words, "where Nature spread so rich a mantle under the eye."

. . . and our own dear Monticello, where has Nature spread so rich a mantle under the eye? mountains, forests, rocks, rivers. with what majesty do we there ride above the storms! how sublime to look down into the workhouse of nature, to see her clouds, hail, snow, rain, thunder, all fabricated at our feet! and the glorious Sun, when rising as if out of a distant water, just gilding the tops of the mountains, & giving life to all nature!

Thomas Jefferson to Maria Cosway, Paris, October 12, 1786[1]

This book results from our love of Monticello and its endlessly inspiring beauty—in daring compositions, eloquent details, and sweeping vistas—across differing hours and seasons. As we questioned how to capture this wonder on pages, Gil Schafer III and Philip Reeser offered invaluable support. Together the four of us envisioned a book by those who shared Thomas Jefferson's passion for arts and culture, professionals in each of the endeavors he pursued in his bid to create the wondrous and all-encompassing "curiosity of the neighborhood"[2] that is Monticello—house, plantation, and landscape. We insisted that Gil pick up his pen on behalf of architecture. We knew of only one photographer worthy of revealing the incomparable eye of Thomas Jefferson—Miguel Flores-Vianna. Miguel and his assistant Brett Thomas Wood spent many days and dawn hours capturing images that are without doubt the finest visual compendium ever assembled of Monticello. How the sage of the little mountain would have been enthralled with the art and science of their genius.

We are deeply indebted to Miguel and the celebrated authors, all of whom shared our vision and donated their work as a gift to Monticello. One might quip from John Kennedy's testament to Nobel Prize laureates gathered for dinner at the White House, and speculate that never has so much talent been assembled for Monticello in one place, "with the possible exception of when Thomas Jefferson dined [here] alone."[3] To Miguel Flores-Vianna, Annette Gordon-Reed, Carla Hayden,

Gil Schafer III, Xavier F. Salomon, Jay McInerney, Alice Waters, Thomas Woltz, and Jon Meacham, we offer profound gratitude. Jon Meacham has repeatedly said that the closest one can come to having a conversation with Thomas Jefferson is to visit Monticello. With the help of these luminaries, that conversation is even more revealing and visual, and now acknowledges the critical roles and work of the enslaved who made Monticello possible. We must never lose sight of how Monticello was created.

We owe special thanks and recognition to our publisher Charles Miers and associate publisher Margaret Rennolds Chace, who nurtured this project with special care. Our editor Philip Reeser opened every door and assembled the dream team for its production, including the "best"—Jason Best, our copy editor; Alyn Evans, our production manager; Nicki Clendening, our publicity coordinator; and Richard Slovak, our proofreader. We are especially fortunate that Philip recommended the eloquent eye and hand of Jesse Kidwell for the book's design.

Many Monticello colleagues played a critical role in supporting the research and logistics of this book, on top of their normal duties, and often at inconvenient times. We wish to thank and offer credit to curators, collections and restoration specialists Gardiner Hallock, Susan Stein, Lucy Midelfort, Emilie Johnson, Diane Ehrenpreis, Tabitha Corradi, Malia Sbach, Caitlin Bowes, Kathy Garstang, Sam Schmucker, Jolen Bain, and Carol Richardson; historians and librarians Ann Lucas, Niya Bates, Anna Berkes, Endrina Tay, and Brandon Dillard; archaeologists Derek Wheeler, Crystal O'Connor, and Alison Mueller; gardens experts Gabriele Rausse, Jason Young, Peggy Cornett, and Eric Lord; facilities staff Roger Rothwell, Steve Bryant, Carlos Bramhall, Allan Kagan, Kevin Bargy, Lori Allan, and Megan Haynes; education, visitor programs, and guest services staff Gary Sandling, Linnea Grim, Steve Geis, Steve Light, Rachel Baum, Gayle Jessup White, Alyson DeBondt, Dave Blumenstock, and Fred O'Brien; retail and café staff Stephen Ninneman and David Givens; and president's office staff Alexandra Rodriguez and Maeve Jones.

At the helm, coordinating this far-flung cast of luminaries while juggling internal logistics, roles, and deadlines, were Lucy Macon and Tasha Stanton. This book is the beneficiary of their grace and commitment to our vision.

LESLIE GREENE BOWMAN AND
CHARLOTTE MOSS

1   Thomas Jefferson to Maria Cosway, October 12, 1786, in *The Papers of Thomas Jefferson*, ed. Julian P. Boyd (Princeton, NJ: Princeton University Press, 1954), 10:443–55.

2   Thomas Jefferson to Frederick W. Hatch, May 12, 1822, Coolidge Collection of Thomas Jefferson Manuscripts, Massachusetts Historical Society. Full quotation reads, "Experience has proved to me that my place is considered as among the curiosities of the neighborhood, and that it will probably be visited as such by most of the attendants."

3   John F. Kennedy, "Remarks at a Dinner Honoring Nobel Prize Winners of the Western Hemisphere," April 29, 1962. Published by Gerhard Peters and John T. Woolley, eds., *American Presidency Project*. Full quotation reads, "I think this is the most extraordinary collection of talent, of human knowledge, that has ever been gathered together at the White House, with the possible exception of when Thomas Jefferson dined alone."

ANNETTE GORDON-REED is the Carl M. Loeb University Professor at Harvard. Gordon-Reed has won sixteen book prizes, including the Pulitzer Prize in History in 2009 and the National Book Award in 2008, for *The Hemingses of Monticello: An American Family*.

CARLA HAYDEN was sworn in as the 14th Librarian of Congress on September 14, 2016. Hayden is the first woman and the first African American to lead the national library. Hayden was formerly the chief executive officer of the Enoch Pratt Free Library in Baltimore and is a past president of the American Library Association.

JAY McINERNEY is the author of twelve books, most recently *Bright, Precious Days* (2016). He writes a monthly wine column for *Town & Country* and was previously the wine columnist for the *Wall Street Journal* and *House & Garden*. In 2006, McInerney won the James Beard M. F. K. Fisher Distinguished Writing Award.

JON MEACHAM is a presidential historian, contributing writer to the *New York Times Book Review*, contributing editor at *Time*, and Pulitzer Prize–winning author. A member of the Council on Foreign Relations and of the Society of American Historians, Meacham holds the Rogers Chair in the American Presidency and is a distinguished visiting professor at Vanderbilt University.

XAVIER F. SALOMON is the Deputy Director and Peter Jay Sharp Chief Curator at The Frick Collection, New York. A noted scholar of Paolo Veronese, he curated the monographic exhibition on the artist at the National Gallery, London (2014). In 2018, Italy named Salomon *Cavaliere dell'Ordine della Stella d'Italia*. In his 2018 book, *Canova's George Washington,* Salomon illuminated Thomas Jefferson's influence on Canova's only American commission.

GIL SCHAFER III is an award-winning architect, consistently recognized as a leading practitioner of contemporary classical architecture. A member of *Architectural Digest*'s AD100, and recipient of *Veranda*'s Art of Design Award and the 2019 Arthur Ross Award in Architecture, he is the author of *The Great American House* (2012) and *A Place to Call Home* (2017).

ALICE WATERS is a chef, author, food activist, and, since 1971, owner of Chez Panisse restaurant in Berkeley, California. She has been a champion of local sustainable agriculture for more than four decades. In 1995, she founded the Edible Schoolyard Project, which advocates for a free regenerative school lunch for all children and a sustainable food curriculum in every public school.

THOMAS WOLTZ is the owner of Nelson Byrd Woltz Landscape Architects. In 2011, Woltz was invested into the American Society of Landscape Architects Council of Fellows, among the highest honors in the profession. In 2013, he was named the Design Innovator of the Year by the *Wall Street Journal Magazine*. His design work infuses places where people live, work, and play with narratives of the land that inspire stewardship.

The Thomas Jefferson Foundation is grateful to a number of donors for their support of restorations at Monticello. A transformational gift from David M. Rubenstein made the most recent restoration campaign possible. Additional leadership gifts were generously provided by Grady and Lori Durham and family for the Cabinet, David and Susan Goode and family for the Bed Chamber, Christopher J. Toomey for the Library, Polo Ralph Lauren for the Dining Room, Charlotte Moss and Barry Friedberg for Martha Jefferson Randolph's Room, the Florence Gould Foundation for the 1809 Kitchen, Howard and Abby Milstein and the Roller-Bottimore Foundation for the Wine Cellar, and Fritz and Claudine Kundrun, the Sarah and Ross Perot, Jr. Foundation, the Richard S. Reynolds Foundation, the Mars family, the National Endowment for the Humanities, Mr. and Mrs. Richard A. Mayo, the Cabell Foundation, Garden Club of Virginia, and the Beirne Carter Foundation for Mulberry Row.

DESCRIPTION OF WORKS

PAGE 4
BUST OF THOMAS JEFFERSON;
    made by Jean-Antoine Houdon;
    patinated plaster; France; 1789; gift
    of the Gilder Lehrman Collection

PAGE 9
TOMBSTONE OF PRISCILLA
    HEMMINGS; made by John
    Hemmings; slate; Monticello; 1830

PAGE 11
MARTHA WAYLES SKELTON
    JEFFERSON'S BOOK OF
    COLLECTED SHEET MUSIC;
    paper, ink, and leather; England
    and United States; 1760–80;
    private collection

PAGE 18
PENDULE CLOCK; designed
    by Thomas Jefferson and made by
    Louis Chantrot; marble, brass,
    and ormolu; Paris; 1790; gift of a
    private collector
JEFFERSON'S TRAVELING PISTOLS;
    made by Charles Freeth; brass and
    wood; London; 1783–4; gift of
    Florence P. Kennedy

PAGE 19
DISPLAY OF NATIVE AMERICAN
    ARTIFACTS; various works
    reproduced by Butch Thunder
    Hawk, Mark McBride, Larry
    Belitz, Walter Black Hoop, and
    Jo Esther Parshall; period artifacts:

gifts of Page Randolph Allen; a
bequest from Charles, James, and
John Eddy; and loans from the
American Numismatic Society
and the Smithsonian Institution's
National Museum of the American
Indian and National Museum of
Natural History

PAGE 22
JEFFERSON'S COPY OF IL
    PETRARCA CON DICHIARAZIONI
    NON PIÙ STAMPATE by Francesco
    Petrarca; paper, leather, and ink;
    France; 1558

205

206

REPRODUCTIONS OF JEFFERSON'S
PORTRAITS OF SIR FRANCIS
BACON AND ISAAC NEWTON
PORTRAIT OF DAVID
RITTENHOUSE; engraved by
Edward Savage, after the painting
by Charles Willson Peale,
Philadelphia, 1796; paper and ink;
Philadelphia; 1796
FORTEPIANO; made by George Astor
& Company; wood and ivory;
London; 1805–12; gift of
Laurence G. Hoes
UPPER RIGHT:
JEFFERSON'S PORTRAIT OF
BENJAMIN FRANKLIN; painted
by Jean Valade; oil on canvas; Paris;
ca. 1786, after original by Joseph
Silfrede Duplessis, Paris, 1778
HARPSICHORD; made by Jacob
Kirckman; wood and ivory;
London; 1762; gift of Patricia M.
Kluge

PAGES 102–103
MARTHA WAYLES SKELTON
JEFFERSON'S BOOK OF
COLLECTED SHEET MUSIC;
paper, ink, and leather; England
and United States; 1760–80;
private collection
HARPSICHORD; made by Jacob
Kirckman; wood and ivory;
London; 1762; gift of Patricia M.
Kluge

PAGE 104
CHESS GAMING PIECES; bone;
possibly England; 1800–40; loaned
by the University of Virginia

PAGE 113
CALASH; silk and metal; probably
England; 1770 -1800; gift of Juliet
Graves Meikleham

PAGE 122
Foreground: DECANTER; leaded glass
(mouth-blown); England; 1750–70
Background: WINE BOTTLE;
unrefined glass (mouth-blown);
England; 1760–80

PAGES 140–141
DINING ROOM MANTELPIECE
(detail); wood, composition, and
jasperware (later replacement);
ca. 1805

PAGE 142
ASKOS; made by Anthony Simmons
and Samuel Alexander; silver;
Philadelphia; 1801; gift of Thomas
Jefferson Coolidge, III

PAGES 144–145
WINE GLASS COOLER; made by
Sèvres Manfactory and decorated
by Geneviève Taillandier;
hard-paste porcelain; France; 1787;
bequest of Juliet Graves
Meikleham
WINE GLASSES; blown glass; England;
ca. 1780; bequest of Margaret
Taylor
SALVER; made by William Hunter;
silver; London; 1751; bequest of
Frances Louise Meikleham
PAIR OF SALTS; made by Elizabeth
Muns; silver; London; ca. 1768
TUMBLER; silver with gold wash;
Paris; ca. 1785; bequest of Charles,
James, and John Eddy
FOUR TUMBLERS; made by John
Letelier; silver with gold wash;
Richmond, Virginia; 1810; gift
of William A. Meikleham; gift of
Margaret Kean Rubel; gift of
the family of Nicholas R. Burke;
and purchase
PAIR OF GOBLETS; made by
Claude-Nicolas Delanoy; silver
with gold wash; Paris; 1789; loaned
by Mrs. Benjamin H. Caldwell and
purchase
SET OF FOUR PLATES; made by
Pierre-Jacques Lamine; silver;
Paris; 1786–7; gift of James
Jackson Storrow; loaned by
Lawrence R. Greenough, Jr. and
Mrs. Elizabeth G. Mullings
PAIR OF COVERED DISHES;
made by Antoine Boullier; silver;
Paris; 1786–7; loaned by
Lawrence R. Greenough, Jr.
and Mrs. Elizabeth G. Mullings,
and purchase

PAGE 149
COFFEE URN; made by Jacques-
Louis-Auguste Leguay; silver;
Paris; 1787–8

PAGE 152
TUREEN AND PLATTER; earthen-
ware; England; ca. 1800; loaned by
the Colonial Williamsburg
Foundation

PAGE 153
LADLE; made by James Tookey; silver;
London; 1764–5

PAGE 154
REPRODUCTION OF BUST OF
BENJAMIN FRANKLIN; patinated
plaster; United States; ca. 1900,
after the original by Jean-Antoine
Houdon, Paris, ca. 1789
BRACKET (one of four); plaster;
possibly Paris; ca. 1789

PAGE 193
JEFFERSON'S RIDING BOOTS;
leather; United States; 1790–1826;
gift of John H. Randolph, Jr.

PAGE 194
JEFFERSON'S NOTEBOOK; ivory and
silver; Philadelphia; ca. 1790;
bequest of Charles, James, and
John Eddy

PAGE 195
JEFFERSON'S POLYGRAPH; made by
John Isaac Hawkins and Charles
Willson Peale; mahogany and
brass; Philadelphia; 1806; loaned
by the University of Virginia

PAGE 197
JEFFERSON'S FROCK COAT; wool
and cotton weave, linen, cotton,
silk, and ivory; United States;
ca. 1800

First published in the United States of America in 2021 by
Rizzoli International Publications, Inc.
300 Park Avenue South
New York, New York 10010
www.rizzoliusa.com

Publisher: Charles Miers
Senior editor: Philip Reeser
Production manager: Alyn Evans
Design coordinator: Olivia Russin
Copy editor: Jason Best
Managing editor: Lynn Scrabis

Editorial assistance and coordination at Monticello provided
by Diane Ehrenpreis, Gardiner Hallock, Lucy Macon, and
Tasha Stanton

Designer: Jesse Kidwell

Photography by Miguel Flores-Vianna
Texts by Annette Gordon-Reed, Carla Hayden,
Jay McInerney, Jon Meacham, Xavier F. Salomon,
Gil Schafer III, Alice Waters, and Thomas Woltz

A portion of Jay McInerney's
"An Appreciation of the Grape" was originally published
in the December 3, 2006, edition of the *New York Times* as
"The Founding Wine Geek."
© 2006 The New York Times Company. All rights reserved.
Used under license.

ISBN: 978-0-8478-6522-2
Library of Congress Control Number: 2021935977

2021 2022 2023 2024 / 10 9 8 7 6 5 4 3 2 1

Printed and bound in China

Facebook.com/RizzoliNewYork
Twitter: @Rizzoli_Books
Instagram.com/RizzoliBooks
Pinterest.com/RizzoliBooks
Youtube.com/user/RizzoliNY
Issuu.com/Rizzoli